02.13.09

Chandra,

We walk where
we watch, so
look to Jesus!

Val

Tainted Mirror
An Anthology

Edited and compiled by

Valerie L. Coleman

Published by

Pen of the Writer, LLC

5523 Salem Avenue
Dayton, Ohio 45426
PenoftheWriter.com

Published by

Pen of the Writer, LLC
5523 Salem Avenue
Dayton, Ohio 45426
PenoftheWriter.com
info@PenoftheWriter.com

Pen of the Writer, LLC is a Christian publishing company committed to using the writing pen as a weapon to fight the enemy and celebrate the good news of Christ Jesus.

Library of Congress Control Number: 2007937171

ISBN-13: 978-0-9786066-1-9

Cover design by Candace K CanDann.com

Printed in the United States of America

Praise for
Tainted Mirror An Anthology...

"When life leaves you weary, worn and weathered, buckling under its grueling weight is expected. *Standing*, on the other hand, is born of pure will as the powerfully inspiring stories in *Tainted Mirror An Anthology* demonstrate. Topics ranging from the personal battle of imprisonment or empowerment, faith and forgiveness, choice versus chance, attest to the human spirit's ability to discern and rise above any and all hurdles.

Valerie L. Coleman has done an outstanding job of harmonizing several authentic lessons of endurance and overcoming that flow from the pens of a refreshing league of authors."

Dr. Vivi Monroe Congress
Author of *The Bankrupt Spirit* and *Manna for Mamma: Wisdom for Women in the Wilderness*
DrViviMonroeCongress.com

"In *Tainted Mirror An Anthology*, Valerie L. Coleman delves into issues that keep us from dying to self and experiencing abundant life. If you are ready to do whatever it takes to walk into your purpose, these insightful and encouraging stories will lead you there."

Stephanie Robinson
Author of *Anointed to Die*
StephanieRobinsonMinistries.org

I dedicate this book to my Passionate Pens. They inspired and encouraged me to compile this book on their behalf and ended up ministering to my heart.

From Thurgood Marshall High School
    Jessica D. Allen
    José Omar Gutierrez
    Christopher D. Lyttle

From Dayton Correctional Institution
    Charles E. Loper, III
    Brian Revere
    Charles "Chill Will" Williams

For I know the thoughts that I think toward you, saith the Lord, thoughts of peace, and not evil, to give you an expected end.
~ Jeremiah 29:11

Proceeds from book sales will be applied to the Passionate Pens Scholarship Fund. The money will be used to teach writing and publishing to high school students and fund the free/discounted books supplied to prison inmates.

Passionate Pens

Acknowledgements

In addition to my Lord and Savior Jesus Christ, husband, children, parents, sister and Meme's babies, I must also acknowledge

o Christopher McNeal, Christopher Reid and Christopher Surratt of Christopher Entertainment Group. You helped me through my most trying journey and for that I will be forever grateful. Know you! Do you!
o Franklin R. Simpson, God bless your bones.
o Dr. Vivi Monroe Congress, my accountability partner and confidant.
o Sheree Welch, my friend and HP consultant. Jesus, keep us near the cross!
o Anthony and Lisa Vaughn for praying me through my wilderness.
o Darnell "Tha REPresenta" Alexander for listening to the Spirit and sending words of encouragement.
o Avalon Betts-Gaston, Esquire for giving me sound legal guidance.
o My Soul of the Pen sisters — Marcella Ashe, LaTonya Branham, Kaye Jeter, Gail Miller and Dorinda Nusum.
o Warden Lawrence Mack and Vivian Covington for giving me the approval and support to teach at the Dayton Correctional Institution.
o Charlotte Chinn, publisher of *Solo Parenting,* for typing the inmates' submissions. SoloParenting@yahoo.com
o Mark and Tonya Baker of the Mark Baker Foundation for seeing the vision of the Passionate Pens.
o And of course the anthology contributors.

Table of Contents

Introduction

When the students and inmates of the Passionate Pens program asked me to publish them in a book, I intended to focus on how we look at life through tainted eyes — image, prestige, money, popularity — at the expense of integrity, peace of mind and a victorious life. I planned to delve into training your mind to look beyond your circumstance and dwell on those things that are good, pure and lovely.

I anticipated persuading you to replace the negative thoughts that bombard you daily. I desired to convince you to shut out the words and actions of others and evoke you to break free of their opinions to walk in your purpose. I planned to encourage you to stop looking in the past, but rather to the future because we walk in the direction we watch.

I had hoped to explain how the Lord used liars, cheaters and murderers to fulfill His purpose in biblical times and that He still does today. I wanted to mention that the children of Israel were released from Pharaoh's physical captivity, but remained in bondage to their minds. I decided to include Scriptures about the tongue being the smallest, yet deadliest member and how we speak what's in our hearts to drive home the power of confession. I expected to lead you to passages that dwelt on renewing the mind and knowing that God has great plans for you.

I did *not* expect to be thrust into a wilderness as a martyr for the cause. But the Lord's thoughts are not my thoughts and His ways — you already know. So before I could compile this book on freedom from captivity, I had to be taken hostage and then released! Glory to His name!

Valerie L. Coleman

My Prayer

Oh, Lord,
teach me to profit and lead me
by the way that I should go.

Extracted from Isaiah 48:17b

Vehicular Homicide
By Valerie L. Coleman

No matter what time she awoke, Jeanie always ended up rushing to get her children to the bus stop on time. She ran into the kitchen to pack lunches for her husband, David, and daughters, who sat at the table eating breakfast. She rummaged through the drawers in search of a sandwich baggie.

"Babe, don't forget to take the girls to ballet practice," she said to her husband, as she slapped jelly on the bread. "I've got a late meeting today."

"Got it in my PDA," David said, as he put peaches in the girls' *Dora the Explorer* lunch totes. "So I'll see you around six?"

"Yeah. I'll pick up dinner." Jeanie bobbed her head in the direction of the garage.

David grabbed his briefcase and chuckled. "I know. A two-car garage and I'm parking in the driveway. I'll clean it this weekend." He kissed his wife, hugged his girls and then left out the front door.

Jeanie wiped the sweat from her brow. She turned to her twin daughters who slurped the milk from their bowl of cereal. "Come on girls. Time to go." The trio jogged to the corner and arrived as the last child stepped onto the bus. "Okay, ladies," she sighed, "have a good day. Protection in the name of Jesus."

"Bye, Mommy. We love you." Jeanie kissed the girls and then trotted home.

Already behind schedule, she grabbed her keys and ran into the garage. She jumped in the car and popped *Christopher's* newest release, *The Journey*, into the CD player. She skipped to her favorite track, *Yes*. With the hectic start to her day, she needed to usher in the Lord's presence fast.

"Father, I thank You for another day." She petitioned her Daddy for His will as she drove to work. Deep in prayer, and inattentive to her surroundings, she failed to navigate a hair-pin turn. She overcompensated and crossed to the opposite side of the isolated two-lane highway. The tires spun without restraint in the loose gravel and the 2005 Impala skid out of control. "The blood of Jesus!" Jeanie threw up her hands to shield herself as the vehicle bounded down the steep ravine. The dense foliage shrouded the car as it came to rest in a shadowed gully.

An hour later, still delirious from the impact, Jeanie opened her eyes. She leaned back on the headrest and waved away the imaginary birds that fluttered around her. As she ran her hands over her body to check for broken bones, a bolt of pain seared through her chest. She struggled to unfasten the seatbelt. The clasp had jammed.

"Oh, my God!" Frantic, she reached for her cell phone. "Still on the charger. Jesus!" Tears raced down her cheeks. She grabbed a travel pack of tissue from the console and dabbed at her face. "Okay, get yourself together." She tried to open the door, but tree branches pressed against the car and sealed it shut. Trapped. Her heart pounded as she realized no one would look for her in the secluded place.

"Lord, I know that You have given me the spirit of power, love and a sound mind, but right now, I am scared. I don't know how I got in this place and I don't know how I'm going to get out." With her breathing labored, she continued. "I'm trapped in this pit with no way to call for help. Why are You doing this to me?" She slammed her fists against the dashboard. "This is not fair!" She clutched her chest in an attempt to alleviate the pain and then passed out.

~ ~ ~ ~ ~ ~ ~

In the third hour, Jeanie opened her eyes. As the dizziness subsided, she remembered the small metal hammer in the glove compartment. She grabbed the tool and unscrewed the handle to expose a flathead screwdriver. She jabbed the screwdriver into the seatbelt clasp. She stabbed her hand several times and then tried to use the screwdriver as a knife to cut the seatbelt. She continued until the sweat and blood flowed together. Futile.

"Lord, You promised that You would never leave me. I know Your Word to be true, so why do I feel as though You've abandoned me?" She grabbed the steering wheel and jerked her body back and forth. "Do You hear me, God? Do You even care?"

After several tugs on the seatbelt, it released. She lifted her blouse to find a large black and blue bruise that seemed to spread before her eyes. "Oh, God! Not like this. I don't want to die like this!"

~ ~ ~ ~ ~ ~ ~

Hours into her struggle to live, Jeanie resolved to trust the Lord. "This is not how I had planned to go, but if it be Your will that I die now, then so be it." As she accepted her destiny, peace filled her heart. A deer walked in front of the car. It paused, tilted its head, looked at Jeanie and then pranced away.

The shafts of sunlight that peeked through the green canopy narrowed as night approached. She smiled as she thought about the last game of Hide and Seek she played with her babies. In a sing-song voice, she mimicked, "'Mommy, where are you? Come out, come out wherever you are.'"

Bright lights flashed. "I can hear my girls calling to me. Oh Lord, please protect my darlings." Jeanie prepared for the worst and closed her eyes.

15

"Daddy, she's in here!" The girls chimed in unison as they flicked the garage lights on and off.

David ran to the car still parked in the garage. He flung open the door and offered his hand to Jeanie. "Dying to your flesh again, huh?"

"Yeah." She took his hand and stepped out of the car. Her knees buckled.

"I got you," he said, as he grabbed her around the waist.

"Submitting to His will is a lot of work. I get so consumed, I lose track of everything. What time is it?"

"Eight." He closed the car door and assisted Jeanie up two steps to the laundry room. "The girls and I called everyone." He kissed her on the cheek. "And you've been in the garage the whole time." He helped Jeanie to the kitchen table, pulled out a chair for her and then walked to the refrigerator.

"Well, the Bible says mortify, not pacify, the flesh." The girls ran to her and smothered her with hugs and kisses. "How are Momma's girls? How about pizza tonight?"

The girls jumped up and down several times. "Yah!" They ran into the family room to watch Nickelodeon.

Jeanie called in the order and then shuffled through the mail piled on the table. She paused and looked at her husband. "You know, this prayer was different."

He placed a glass of ice water on the table and then sat next to his wife. "How so?"

She told him about the experience and then elaborated. "First of all, the ravine was a dark pit comparable to my wilderness experience, my hell on earth. Like the Lord had to take me to a low place, almost near death, to resurrect me in His glory. But then the love of Christ covered me." She guzzled down the water and then set the glass on the table.

"You mean the trees and such that covered the car?" David rested his elbow on the table and then leaned toward his wife.

"Yeah."

"No weapon formed against you."

"Exactly. The trees were massive, deep-rooted and firm. They did not budge and kept the car from going further into the pit." She tore open the telephone bill. "I was shut in the car like Noah in the ark — my secret place."

"Hmm, interesting." He rubbed his goatee.

"What?"

"The trees. They could represent the True Vine, Jesus. You know like in John 15. The Husbandman was looking to see if you were a branch that bore fruit."

"Well, I tell you what, if I wasn't a fruit-bearer before this experience, I sure am now." She inhaled and released a deep breath. "I was thinking more like the trees represented the cross and His requirement for me to die to my flesh daily."

"Both work. Jesus was the ultimate fruit on the tree when He hung on the cross."

"Uh-huh. That's good." Jeanie picked up the glass and swirled the ice around in it. "Now the seatbelt was my own unwillingness to release the hurt and yield to Him. I held myself in bondage. My stubbornness and rebellion kept me imprisoned. It forced the Lord to work even harder on my heart and thus the bruise on my chest."

"Wow, that's deep."

"I know it. Can you believe that?" She walked into the family room to check on the girls and then returned to the kitchen.

"Isolated in a forestry wilderness, I had to go through this process alone — only God and me. No one else could walk this walk for me, but me. I had to trust Him to lead me through even though I could not see my way out." A tear rolled down her cheek and David wiped it away with the back of his hand. "And just before I died, a deer pranced up to the car — my present-day ram in the bush."

"Like the song goes, you finally reached the point where your soul longed after Him like the deer pants for water." He shook his head. "That's just awesome."

"The presence of the Lord was with me in my wilderness. Although the experience bruised my flesh, I was not destroyed by the Lord's pruning process. He worked the mess out of me without annihilating me. Like the potter with his clay and the silversmith with his precious metal, He kept a watchful eye. Never turning away or applying too much pressure. He knew that without proper attention, His work of art would become useless waste." Jeanie looked at the clock on the stove and then the front door. "Where's that pizza?"

"So what happened when you finally gave up your will for His?"

"When I rose out of my wilderness, brightness overpowered me. The glory of the Lord shone through and swallowed up the darkness. He revealed to me that when I yield my will to His, He takes full responsibility for the outcome. He provided light to show me the escape route. He ordered my steps."

David chuckled. "That was the girls playing with the lights."

"Whatever. I say it was the Lord's majestic presence. That's my story and I'm sticking to it."

False Identity
By Jessica D. Allen

Darkness consumed the daylight as the sun descended from the heavens. The streets overflowed with lovers of money, pleasure and themselves. Jasmine strolled past crack heads drenched in their favorite colognes of alcohol and marijuana. Engulfed in her recent sexual encounter, she heard her lover's voice. *You're the only one for me. I love you, Jazzi.* She turned around hoping to gaze into his eyes, only to find that her thoughts had betrayed her again.

She sat on a bench with her head cupped in her hands trying to block out memories from her childhood. With a glimmer of light from the lamppost above her head; Jasmine reached in her bag for the red notebook that contained her innermost thoughts. She fumbled with the ruffled pages as she looked for a clean sheet. Jasmine ran her fingers through her long brown hair. Tears fell from her hazel eyes as she tapped her pen. Her emotions rippled across the notebook as her pen embodied her thoughts and stained the page. *Don't hold back just because it hurts. Write away...*

Five minutes later, a young man yelled out, "Hey you!"

Jasmine continued to let her soul pour out onto the wrinkled pages.

"Hey you!"

She looked up at the chubby, bothersome man driving the RTA bus.

"Are you riding the bus or what?"

"Oh sorry, I was caught up in my own little world." She grabbed her bag and got on the bus.

"That'll be $1.25."

"I have a pass." She slid the card through the slot and then stuffed it in her pocket. "Thank you." She scurried to the back of the bus and continued to let her heart speak. A few stop lights and speed bumps later, Jasmine signed and dated her journal entry. She placed the book in her bag and then signaled the driver to stop.

"You have a nice night, young lady."

"Nice night? Not at my house." She said as she got off the bus.

Jasmine leaned on a raggedy fence while a heavy breeze blew debris that settled under her feet. She walked toward her personal house of terror. Filled with so many horrifying memories, she couldn't bare to go inside. Her heart raced so fast it sounded like a collegiate drum line. As she walked up the stairs, agonizing spasms shot through her body. Her hands trembled and sweat beaded on her forehead. Just as she reached for the knob, the door swung open. Jasmine turned, tripped down the steps and fell on the wet grass.

Aaron, Jasmine's brother, a milk chocolate Adonis, ran to her and then squatted to look into her eyes. "Jazzi, it's me."

Tears flowed down her flawless face. "I thought you were h---"

"I know, sweetie," he said as he helped her up.

Jasmine punched Aaron in his chest. "We need to get out of this house. I can't stand being here."

"Where are we going to go? Our family doesn't even cl---"

Their disgruntled father stood on the porch. "Aaron, get in this house now!"

"Come on, we better get inside," he said and wrapped his arms around her.

"Jasmine, is that you?" her father asked, as his stealth six-foot-two frame walked to the top step.

"Yeah, Andrew it's me."

"Now what I did tell you about calling me Andrew? I'm your daddy."

She sucked her teeth and rolled her eyes. "Andrew is the name your mother gave you, so I'm gonna call you by your birth name. You got a problem with that?"

He yanked her arm and tightened his lips. "I don't know who you think you are." Jasmine tried to pull away, but he spun her around to face him. "You better look at me when I'm talking to you."

She snatched away from his grip and looked at Aaron. "Yeah, whatever. When was the last time you cleaned yourself up? You look like a homeless man begging for loose change."

Aaron chuckled.

"Girl, you better shut your mouth. Now go upstairs before I do something that I might get locked up for."

The siblings darted upstairs as if they were inches from the finish line of a neck-and-neck race. Jasmine went into Aaron's room and plopped on his half-made bed. She picked up his cell phone and scrolled through his text messages. Seconds later, Aaron came through the door. Guilt covered Jasmine's face like Steve Urkel during one of his "Did I do that?" moments.

"What are you doing?" He grabbed his phone and slid it in his pocket.

"Nothing, I was just looking at it. When did you get a Motorola Razor?"

He stretched out across his bed and rested his head on Jasmine's thigh. "A friend gave it to me." He lifted his right eyebrow. "So, where have you been all night?"

"I was… Um, at a friend's house."

"Do I know this *friend*?" He massaged his chin.

"No. He's, I mean ---"

"What? I thought you were at your girlfriend's house!" Aaron sat up and glared at his sister.

"Aaron, calm d---"

"Calm down! Girl, you must be outside your mind. What were you doing at some wanna be thug's house?"

She thought back on what had happened hours earlier. They had fulfilled their lustful desires, however she left with a half-empty glass of temporary satisfaction. Jasmine gazed out the window, as she hesitated to reply.

"What were you doing at his house?"

"Nothing. We were just watching *Romeo Must Die.*"

"Why were you out so late? It's almost midnight and you had me worried." He pulled up his left sleeve revealing his ripped biceps and a new tattoo. "It's my job to look out for my baby sister."

She traced the fancy lettering on his arm. "'I'm my sister's keeper.' You got this for me?"

"Not just for you, but to remind me that I have to protect you at all costs." He rolled down his sleeve. "Want to go to church with me tomorrow?"

"Uh-no, not really. Why?"

"My friend visited this new church and she sa--"

"Oh, so you can have friends of the opposite sex but I can't."

"You can have friends. You just can't be friendly with 'em." They chuckled. "I'm serious though, why don't you want to go?

"I'd feel weird going to church after all these years. Besides God's never done anything miraculous for me, so why bother?"

"Wait a minute. Just because your faith isn't what it used to be, doesn't mean He hasn't done anything for you."

22

"What has He done for me, Aaron?" She kicked off her shoes and sat Indian style on the bed. "Honestly, I have no clue."

"He's given you life."

She crinkled her nose and looked up at the ceiling.

"I know you're not happy with your life right now, but if you give Him a chance He can turn your situation around." He rubbed her arm. "All you have to do is believe. He'll take it from there."

"I have so much anger built up inside of me I can't do it."

"Well, I don't care what you say." He shrugged. "You're going to church with me tomorrow."

"No, I don't want to--"

"Jazzi, you're going to have to come face-to-face with reality or you'll continue to walk in darkness. Now go take a shower and get to bed."He pushed her off the bed. "You're going tomorrow."

She walked toward the door, turned and then saluted. "Sir, yes sir."

"Hey, Jazzi. I love you."

"I love you too, bighead."

~ ~ ~ ~ ~ ~ ~

The vivid sunlight streamed through the window and pierced Jasmine's eyes. She squinted, rolled on her side and tried to fall back asleep. Seconds later, Aaron rushed into her room.

"Jasmine, get up and put on some clothes."

"What time is it?"

"It's nine. We're already a half-hour late for church. Come on let's go."

"All right, all right. I'll get dressed." Jasmine groaned and then wiped the sleep out of her eyes. "What should I wear?"

"Your clothes are lying on your dresser."

"So what, you're my wardrobe man now?"

"Yeah, that's right. Now hurry up."

Jasmine slipped a pair of South Pole jeans over her shapely legs. The coordinated orange and white button-up accentuated her caramel tone. She slid her size-seven feet into some fresh-out-the-box Air Force Ones and walked down the stairs. Aaron stood at the front door tapping his foot. His purple pinstriped Stacy Adams suit hugged his rock-hard frame. He stroked his hand over his thick, wavy hair as Jasmine made her way to front door.

She put her hands on her hips. "Who are you and what did you do with my brother? I like that suit. Where did you get it?"

"I took it from Andrew."

"Is he still here?" She glanced in the mirror and made minor adjustments to her hair.

"Yeah, he's sleeping in his office. I think he had a bad day at work yesterday. Smells like he smoked some weed." Aaron held open the front door for Jasmine. "It took you twenty minutes to get ready. I know one thing; I'm not taking you anywhere else. Get in the car." He playfully pushed her and then hit her upside the head.

"Hey, I just got done fixing my hair."

He shook his head. "I tell you, girls and their hair."

He opened the passenger door of his Toyota Camry. "Buckle up." He jogged to the other side of the car, put the key in the ignition and hurried down the street.

"How far is this church anyway?"

"It's not too far. Maybe ten or fifteen minutes away."

Jasmine looked at the dashboard clock. "Well, it's 9:20 now. So by the time we get there we're only going to hear the last fifteen minutes of the message."

"That's all it takes to change your life." Aaron cranked up *Clap* and sang along with *Christopher*. He weaved in and out of the Sunday morning traffic on Gettysburg and made a left onto Oakridge. He parked in the first available spot a couple of blocks down the street from Vision Christian Fellowship. They jogged toward the front entrance.

Aaron looked back at Jasmine who trailed behind him. "Will you pick up the pace?"

"I'm not trying to scuff up my new shoes because you're trying to see your friend."

"Girl, bye." He grabbed her hand and pulled her along.

Two greeters welcomed them with hugs, as an usher found them seats on a back pew. Young people testified to the goodness of God by waving their hands. Pastor Williams, thirty-three and full of the Word, stood at the podium. He looked out into the congregation.

"It's not by circumstance or happenstance that you walked through those doors on this beautiful day that the Lord has made. I have a message from the Father and I don't care if you like or not. Turn in your Bibles to Colossians 3:5-6." He waited for the page rustlings to silence. "'Put to death, therefore, whatever belongs to your earthly nature: sexual immorality, impurity, lust, evil desires and greed, which is idolatry. Because of these, the wrath of God is coming.'" He looked up from his Bible and peered into the congregation. Agitated, Jasmine squirmed in her seat.

"The Word is warning you who indulge in the lust of your flesh that His wrath is coming. If you remain stubborn and don't take heed, you will destroy your chances of getting into Heaven. Stop engaging in premarital sex. Repent before the Lord and abstain from sexual immorality." He sipped from a glass of ice water and then returned it to the podium shelf.

25

"Someone has been hurt beyond comprehension and they are trying to heal their wounds through fornication. Will you come to the altar and give your problems to the Lord? He's tugging on your heart. Don't be afraid. You've been gone long enough."

Jasmine felt a twinge in the pit of her stomach. She desired to know God for herself, but she couldn't help but revert to the helpless little girl that lived inside of her. Overwhelmed with fear, she cried. *Stop! Get off of me. Please.* Memories from that horrible night flooded her mind like the waters that overflowed New Orleans during Hurricane Katrina. Her heart was overtaken with desperation. Jasmine's jumbled thoughts collided into each other. *What are you doing here? You're not thinking about trusting God are you? He let you down, remember?* Rattled by confusion, she dashed out of the sanctuary and ran to Aaron's car.

Aaron ran after her and was almost clipped by an oncoming car. When he caught up to her, he bent over with his hands on his knees and gasped for air. "What happened in there?"

"I can't do it. I've been hurt too much and I just can't open myself to trust anyone."

"Wait a minute. You think Pastor Williams was talking about you?"

She leaned on the car as Aaron opened the door. "Please don't be mad at me. I haven't been honest with you."

"What? About last night?"

"Yeah, I had---"

"Let me guess, you had sex."

"Yeah, I did," she looked down at her feet.

"Look at me, Jasmine." He placed the back of his hand under her chin and lifted her head. "No one is perfect. I need

26

you to understand that I'm not judging you or your actions. That's up to God and God alone."

"Thanks for not coming down on me."

Aaron shook his head. "Don't think you're getting off that easy. I want you to think about your decisions and their consequences. Think before you act."

"I thought that it would make the pain disappear, but it's only making me feel worse. I'll do better. I promise." She rubbed her stomach to stifle the growling. "I'm hungry. Can you stop somewhere?"

"Sure. There's a McDonald's right around the corner. Watch your leg." He closed the door.

After picking up a couple of Big Macs, Aaron dropped Jasmine off at the house. "Hey, I'll be right back. I have to run to the store. Make sure Andrew doesn't touch my food." He pulled out of the driveway.

On her way to the kitchen, she caught a glimpse of her dad, drunk in his office. Rage ignited the adrenaline that raced through her veins. "Humph, I'm not surprised." She placed the food on the kitchen table and took a seat. As she sorted through the bag of burgers, Jasmine was startled by hot breath on the back of her neck. The odor of vodka, rum, and marijuana masked the aroma of her piping hot French fries. She turned to face her frail, unloving father.

"Where have you been?" Andrew slapped her across the cheek.

Jasmine and the food sailed across the room and the pop spilled onto the floor. "I was with Aaron." She rubbed her face and then faltered as she tried to get off the floor. "We went to c-church."

"Church? You think God is going to help you now? You're gonna pay for that attitude you gave me yesterday." He assisted her off the floor by yanking her shirt collar.

"No!" She fought to hold back her tears. "I'm not going to let you beat me anymore."

"Oh, really?" He punched her in the eye. "You've been letting me do it for the past nine years so, what makes today any different?"

The more she pleaded for him to stop, the more Andrew beat her. When he tired, he sat down and picked through the food sprawled on the table.

Aaron came through the door and saw Jasmine laying face down on the floor. He raced to her and slipped on the wet floor. He landed on his back, rolled over and then crawled to her on all fours.

"Jasmine, are you okay?" He turned her over and rested her head in his lap. "I should've taken you with me." He tightened his jaw and balled his fists as he looked at his father. "What is your problem? Why mu---"

Jasmine looked up at her brother and touched his arm. "I want to ask him." Aaron stood and then assisted her to her feet. With her heart filled with despair, she looked at her abuser. "Why do you hate me so much?"

"Hate? You don't know the meaning of the word, but it's time for you to know the truth." Andrew rubbed his scruffy beard and then chuckled. "Your stupid mama. She's the one to blame."

"Don't talk about my mother," Jasmine said as she wiped blood off of her bottom lip.

"I can talk about that dirty slut all I want." In a nonchalant manner, he continued. "She slept with another man and tricked me into believing that you were my child. And when her guilt wouldn't allow her any peace, she left you; both of you. Your mama, my Nicole, didn't want to be your mother or my wife."

Confusion and disbelief stirred on Jasmine's face. "You're lying!" Tears cascaded down her bruised cheek. "My mother would never abandon me!"

Aaron shook his head. "You sick... I'm gonna let you see just how it feels to get beat down." As he lunged at Andrew, Jasmine collapsed and crumpled to the floor. Instead of swinging on Andrew, Aaron turned to Jasmine. "Jasmine, wake up." He picked up her limp body and laid her on the couch. He ran into the kitchen, glaring at Andrew, and wet a paper towel. He placed it on her forehead and then shook her shoulders. "Jasmine, wake up. Please get up!" He leaned over her, prayed and then whispered in her ear. "I'm always going to be here for you no matter what."

Jasmine's body remained still while her mind went on a journey. Surrounded by dilapidated buildings and dented trash dumpsters, she walked through the darkness. In a tattered pair of jeans and red sweatshirt, she sat on the cold pavement and shook like a crack addict aching for the next high. Prostitutes strolled through the alley and waited for midnight Johns. Jasmine wondered how they could freely give what she fought to keep from her molester.

Jasmine thought that giving her life to Him would mean the end of the molestation; the end of her suffering. But as the abuse continued, she felt that God had failed her and the gradual decline in her faith began. Now, at fifteen years old, she found herself at a crossroad and unsure of which path to take. She remembered her mother's last words, *God always takes care of you.*

Ten minutes later, Jasmine woke up. She heard Aaron on the phone with a 911 operator. The paper towel fell off her forehead as she tried to sit up on the couch. She revisited her mother's words and realized that God had kept her all these years. Even though she had gone astray, He loved her. She rolled off the couch and onto the floor. Prostrate before the Lord, she converted the living room into an altar and cried out to God. He understood her moans and groans as she released the pain that had kept her bound. Through her utterances, she repented for all her past sins. She told her Daddy that she was tired of looking to men to fill her emptiness. She asked Him to heal her wounds and love her unconditionally.

"My precious daughter, I will never leave or forsake you."

Drowned in the love of Jesus, she lifted her voice to Heaven and received His presence. For the first time, she felt at home. No one could separate her from the love that God had given her, or at least that's what she thought.

Darkest Days, Brightest Hopes
By José Omar Gutierrez

Lightning struck the lonely night as the sun dissolved into the horizon. Little by little the intensity of the deluge increased as the vicious storm pounded on the little Ohio city. The clustered buildings created a channel for the rain and the abandoned roadway filled as gutters overflowed. Heaven watched as clouds waged war against the wicked earth and drowned it with precipitation.

In the midst of the inclement weather, a man sprinted down the sidewalk. His arms swung like pendulums in harmony with his steps. Moving through the wind, he seemed to elude the rain drops. If it had not been for his drenched clothing, the illusion would have been flawless. Even in the belly of the storm, Edgar Gomez never ceased running.

Despite the chilly rain that beat against his body, his chest was on fire; his stuffy eyes a bloodshot red. Somewhere between the dash from the hospital to now, his tears went astray and became orphans adopted by the wind. His heart felt like it was put over an open flame, and the heaviness of his frown made his face numb. He fixed his stare on the lampposts ahead of him, an attempt to clear his clouded mind, but all he could think about was getting home.

His home, albeit modest, had been his first permanent residence as an adult. He rented the two-room apartment last summer; a place of shelter, security, and fantasy because of his love for his fiancé, Vanessa. Tall and slender with hair that caressed her shoulders, her smooth, dark tone complemented her light eyes. She decorated their home and made sure that everything was in order. The colorful orange walls that once

31

engulfed him in solace, now imprisoned him in memories of her presence and touch. He could no longer sleep in his bed. The sink overflowed with dirty dishes and the hamper stank of worn and re-worn clothes. His loss of strength and determination affected his work ethics and had cost him his job of five years. His hope rested in Vanessa's eyes yet her bouts with deep sleeps, that at times, lasted for days, now hid her once vibrant personality.

Their time together from the night before replayed in his mind as he continued to run. He stared at her as she lay on the hospital bed; the bed that spoke to rumors of death and melancholy. Day after day he sat at her side. He nodded like a bobble-head doll unable to remain in slumber. He gripped her hand tight through the nights awaiting her return; waiting to hear her sweet voice. Her strong, orotund tone resembled his mother's; replenishing and instilling life in him every time she spoke.

"Pray for me," she whispered with a poignant stare. "Pray for us. God always finds a way to bring us closer, to make us stronger. Love is long-suffering, right?"

"Of course," he said with a trembled smile and teary eyes. He leaned over and kissed her.

Edgar seemed to run past time, skip through eternity and remain in forever as he sped past each street. When he arrived at his apartment, he burst through the door and dropped to his knees. Coming to the realization of his exhaustion, he breathed deeply. His hands supported his weight as he squeezed his eyes shut to block out the view of life. Hopeful that his problems disappeared, he opened them. Nothing. Water splattered over the floor as he shook it out of his black hair. He stumbled as he stood and struggled to regain his balance. He paced the room with his head clenched in both hands and ground his teeth.

"What do I do? How did I get here? I'm not ready for this."

The day had plotted against him since the morning. It played in his head like a movie as he continued to pace the desolate room. He screamed with the silence of his sadness.

The Monday started with a brilliant morning sun — warm and full of life — quite different from the downpour and lightning that haunted the night that evening. The pleasant smell of jasmines and glowing daisies in the garden filled his nostrils as he approached the hospital entrance. But the stench of death suffocated his soul as he walked inside. He contemplated going home when a sharp pain struck him in his stomach. He approached the counter.

Man, I must be hungry. Maybe I should get something to eat. He shook the feeling and signed the visitors' log. He thought of spending the usual hour with his fiancé as he scribbled away. The moment he released the pen, the secretary, now standing behind him, pulled him to the side.

"Dr. Sterling wants to speak with you." She directed him to the doctor's office.

Dr. Sterling, or Charles, as they had grown accustomed to calling him, was Vanessa's doctor since day one. A smile molded on his pallid face as he approached the doctor's office. The door opened and Dr. Sterling stepped out alone. His countenance spoke volumes and Edgar's smile vanished.

"I told you that I wasn't sure, but I had a good friend of mine, a neurologist, diagnose her and..." Dr. Sterling paused and then took a deep breath. "We overlooked some symptoms because they weren't as prominent before. They seemed to have arisen overnight. We still can't quite explain how it happened. I... um... we---"

"You what?" Edgar clasped his hands together as if to plead for help. "Charles, tell me what's wrong with my wife!"

"Mr. Gomez," Dr. Sterling said in a soft voice. He reached over and grabbed Edgar by the shoulders. "She has a tumor."

Edgar stepped back to support himself on the wall. He shook his head as tears rushed into his eyes but refused to spill over onto his rosy cheeks.

"No, there must be a mistake. I don't believe you. She can't." Edgar turned away from Dr. Sterling and faced the wall. Unable to respond, the doctor stood and stared at the back of Edgar's head. He wanted to comfort him, but realized his place. He flipped through the pages in his folder.

"We believe it's a mixed neuronal-glial tumor because of its rapid growth. She needs immediate surgery or she will die. We have some of the best brain surgeons on site, but I must be honest with you. Her chances of survival are slim. We have found donors to offset the expense, but you will incur significant out-of-pocket expenses." Reluctant to continue, he dropped his eyes toward the messianic relic that hung on a golden rope from Edgar's neck. He handed Edgar a note card.

Edgar glanced at the card and saw zeros followed by zeros. Without seeing the rest of the digits, he crumbled the card and shoved it deep in his pocket. As he turned to walk away, his pastor, Joshua Bryant, approached. He had visited with Vanessa almost every day since her admission.

"Edgar, I want you to know that we are praying for you and Vanessa. Just wait for your change to come." He touched Edgar's shoulder to console him. Edgar jerked away.

"You've been praying for quite some time now and still nothing. So either you're not getting through to God or He's not listening." Edgar pushed past his spiritual father and ran out of the hospital.

The encounter occurred hours ago yet the memory was as vivid as if it had just happened. He pulled the wet card from his pocket. It had a random design of smeared ink with a trace of zeros too ambiguous to decipher. He threw the crumpled paper to the floor and then sat on the couch. He veiled his face from the light. Sweat rolled from under his forearms and he wept.

"What am I going to do," he whimpered, as he wiped his face. "I don't have that kind of money." Edgar saw a picture of his mother on the dresser. His plans to bring his family out of poverty took second priority to Vanessa's operation. He wished he had the strength of his mother. To her, this situation would be but a simple matter. He stared deep into the eyes of his two-dimensional mother and could almost hear her speak. He stretched his hand out to her like he did when he was in prison. And like in prison, the impenetrable glass wall prevented him from touching his beloved mother. He threw the picture frame on the floor and it shattered.

The hatred that was temporarily doused by the memory of his loving mother revived on impact. With his anger inflamed again, he exploded into a rage. He threw two lamps against the wall. He ravaged his desk and flipped it over. He screamed and pulled his hair. He paced the room and kicked at shards of ceramic and glass.

Thunder struck again as Edgar fell victim to emotional spasms. He dropped to his knees, overturned the coffee table and snatched up the rug underneath it. He pried open the small hatch exposed by the relocated mat. His body froze. His heart shut down and his lungs immobilized. Time itself was altered. He reached into the compartment and pulled out a black 357 Magnum revolver. He blew the accumulated dust particles into the air and wiped it on his wet shirt. Almost a year had past since he had placed it in his palm —grasping it was awkward and condemning. He shrugged and then got to his feet. He placed the gun in the small of his back, tightened his belt and pulled his shirt over his pants.

The rain's intensity diminished to a drizzle and tenderly beat against the window. He walked to the shattered frame and knelt on one knee. He picked up the frame, removed the small pieces of glass attached to it and then placed the picture back on the dresser.

"Perdon a me, ama. True love comes once in a lifetime and I can't let mine slip away." He stood and walked through the door with gun and ambition in possession. As the door crept closed behind him, all other options became a thing of the past.

He looked up and down the street, wiped the drizzling rain from his face and then walked toward the corner. The most illuminated spot in the neighborhood was home to a gas station and convenience store — the perfect location for his plan to unfold. He made a decision and picked the poison to honor his death. For a brief moment, his feet didn't move. Every muscle in his body was paralyzed by the thought of the inevitable. He broke the immobilizing trance, but never moved his focus from the corner store. He took a seat on a dilapidated bench across the street.

Edgar took his ball cap and shook away the loose water. *I'll just walk in there, pretend to buy something and then stick up the guy. That's all, nothing more.* He lifted his jacket collar, tightened it around his ears and attempted to fade into the misty rainfall. *It won't be hard. This store doesn't have any metal gates. It will be perfect.*

Footsteps splashed in puddles and interrupted his thoughts. He refrained from his offensive position at the sight of a group of teenagers approaching the bus stop. Feeling detached from his body, he arose from his seat. He jogged across the street in the little time the crosswalk light allowed, moving the gun from his waist to his front pocket. As Edgar checked to make sure the handle was not exposed, he fixated on his reflection in a puddle. The yellow light from the changing traffic signal bounced off the puddle and snapped him back to the present. He placed his hand on the revolver as he walked by the store window and headed for the entrance. He hesitated in front of the store; the money. He closed his eyes and three gunshots rang in his ear.

Where are the screams? He felt his body come to a halt and then opened his eyes. Instead of the store clerk agonizing in pain, he saw the redness of two brick walls. He didn't do it. Somehow he had walked into the alley between the corner store and another building. Suspicious that others may have seen him, he sought to hide himself from the world.

Attracted to the wall like a magnet to metal, he pushed his back against the brick building. He tried to silence his arduous breathing, but to no avail. His index finger trembled as he raised the revolver to his head. Never before had he felt so ambivalent about stealing. He looked toward the sky with his eyes wide open as the clouds sprinkled rain drops over him.

Wait for your change to come, a voice echoed in his mind. *God may not come when you want him to, but He's always on time.*

The pastor's voice was always a friendly reminder to him that life isn't in his hands. He closed his eyes and lowered the gun. The rain rushed down the side of the building and saturated his back, but he remained pasted against the wall. With a quick flip of his wrist he tossed the gun into the trash can. The gun made a loud noise on contact. It reverberated through the alley and caused the teenagers across the street to look in his direction. Pretending to be ignorant to the source of the noise, he rubbed the back of his head and walked out of the alley. He turned to walk past the store. Afraid to look through the glass door, he dropped his head and hurried past it. Before he knew it, he had crossed the street, sat on the bench and gazed back at the store again. Torn between two worlds, he contemplated suicide only to be born again in the opposite realm.

"Has my own battle of wolves within begun," he said to himself as he sat under the dull street light. "If so, which one am I feeding?"

Edgar sat on the old rotting bench and looked around as if he were waiting for someone to rescue him. He felt foreign to this similar atmosphere; this neighborhood of thieves he once called family. He heard the clamor of shattered glass from break-ins that reminded him of his concealed identity and eroding past. It was different in Mexico. You either stole or drugged yourself so you wouldn't die from hunger. A necessity for survival that wasn't considered a deviant or criminal act like it was here.

His forlorn heart, overwhelmed with the thought of his family back home, bound him; encaged him in guilt. He had promised his mother that he would live a life free of illicit activity, however when he reached the U. S., he took the profession without hesitation. What choice did he have? With no one to support them, he was fueled to take matters into his own hands. He shook his head attempting to loose the blanket of pain that had covered him.

"Hear me out, oh Lord," Edgar mouthed. "Direct me in my path."

He rambled down the street where he and Vanessa had taken up residence. Feeling ashamed and unworthy, he didn't want to return but felt compelled to do so. Blackened clouds still covered the sky as he walked alone in the serenity of the night. Edgar wandered down the gloomy street, while his soul rode the wave of uncertainty crashing against his consciousness. It seemed like yesterday that they strolled down this very sidewalk holding hands. No cares in the world, but to make each other happy. Vanessa was built upon a firm foundation, yet he knew it was only by the grace of God that she still smiled and joked even in the hospital. If only she were here to stabilize him in the areas that only she seemed to reach; his feminine side, he supposed.

"God puts people into our lives for this very reason," he whispered, as he put all movement to a halt. "Our love is but a reflection of Him." Edgar experienced a change of heart. Instead of heading home, he went the opposite direction, toward the pastor's house. The rain had stopped and a mixture of humidity and storm residue set in the atmosphere.

For the first time that night, the moon, bright and dazzling, made its appearance between two dusty clouds. The once bleak night for deviants morphed into a romantic backdrop for lovers. Determined to never let his emotions control him his slow-paced walk accelerated to a jog. He was compelled to apologize to the pastor for his hysterical behavior at the hospital.

~ ~ ~ ~ ~ ~ ~

Earlier that night and several blocks away, Pastor Bryant sat in his home office staring out the window. Fearful that something bad may have happened to Edgar, he dropped his face onto the hardwood desk and mumbled a prayer. Not that it was his fault, but as an overseer, he yearned to do something to help this family. A quick word of encouragement, or even a simple smile could've calmed Edgar. The ring of the doorbell startled him before he could continue in self pity. Pastor Bryant walked to the front door and looked through the peephole.

39

Although he wasn't sure who was standing on his porch, he followed his gut feeling and opened the door with confidence. After a quick reintroduction, Pastor Bryant got a grip of his memory and remembered the tall gray-haired man. He had visited their church about a month back.

The visitor removed his brimmed hat and held it across his chest. "Sorry to catch you so late, but I just couldn't wait any longer to bring this to you. It's for the Hispanic fellow that testified about his ill fiancé. I was the doctor who diagnosed her. I just want to give him this." He extended a crinkled brown paper bag. "Please, if you would, sir."

The pastor, astonished by his unusual behavior, stood with his arms stiff at his side, unable to accept the bag.

"Love is priceless, elder." The aged man said as he placed the bag in Pastor Bryant's large hand. "Well, I have to get going. It's kind of late and my wife is probably worried about me."

As the man went on his way, Pastor Bryant took a look in the paper bag. It was filled with crisp hundred-dollar bills. Excitement embodied Pastor Bryant as relief for Edgar embodied him. "Thank You, Father." Eager to take the money to Edgar, he went for his coat and hat and then grabbed the car keys. He jogged through the drizzle to his silver Audi parked on the street. Before he could duck his head into the car he felt someone behind him. As he turned around, three shots were fired into his stomach.

~ ~ ~ ~ ~ ~ ~

Sirens and flashing lights interrupted Edgar's rhythmic gait. A silver car sped past him and splashed muddy water on his jeans. Fear rose over him and he hastened his pace. As he reached his destination, he found his pastor lying in the street; his blood blending with the pools of water in the gutter. Edgar trembled. He knelt beside his pastor. With great care, he lifted his spiritual father's head and rested it on his lap.

"E-Edgar, is that you?"

"I'm so sorry. This is all my fault."

"No, son, it's not your fault," he coughed and spewed blood. "Reach into my pocket."

Edgar, unable to hold back his tears, shed along with the clouds. He removed the bag from the pastor's coat pocket.

"God never forgets those who love Him," Pastor Bryant reached out and touched Edgar's face. "Remember that."

Edgar, blinded by the array of blue, red and white flashing lights, rested on his knees. He held Pastor Bryant as he took his last breath.

~ ~ ~ ~ ~ ~ ~

Seven months later, with Vanessa recovering well from surgery, Edgar walked with great calmness through the State Penitentiary. His first visit suited and without handcuffs, walking the rocky path surrounded by ten-foot gates and barbed wire revived memories. He rubbed his hands together to dry the clammy moisture on his palms and then stuffed them in the pockets of his black slacks.

"I've got an appointment with Brandon Finkly," Edgar said solemnly. The other guard rung him past security doors and escorted him into the visiting room.

Edgar looked around the large, open room. Artificial plants speckled throughout did little to dim the bright white walls. Two-person tables replete with chairs were positioned every few feet. The air was filled with "I love you" and lamentations from prisoners yearning to leave the wretched place. A tear settled in Edgar's eye. He knew their expressions of sorrow were sincere.

Edgar made his way to an empty table in the middle of the room. Engulfed with anticipation of finally meeting the boy behind the pen, his leg shook under the table. Despite the tragedy surrounding Pastor Bryant, for the past two months Edgar had been corresponding with his murderer weekly.

As he used his finger to trace his name etched in the table, Edgar was unaware of the six-foot-three man standing behind him. He continued to abide in his imagination until Brandon reached over and tapped him on the shoulder.

"Hello, stranger," Brandon said. He smiled as Edgar jumped to his feet and embraced him.

"It's so good to put a face to the penman." Edgar pulled out the other chair and they sat across from each other.

"Sorry that I kept you waiting." Brandon said as he glanced down at the table, scratched his head and then looked back at Edgar. "I was a bit skeptical about you showing up, so I got a little caught up in prayer before I found out you were here."

"It's cool. Don't worry about it," Edgar replied, "You're here now and that's all that matters. Everyone deserves a second chance."

"Thanks, for everything. You are a true friend, Pastor."

Where's God?

By Christopher D. Lyttle

Shareef's dark hand clamped his beloved notebook as his pen scribbled like a mad man with a message. He leaked the soul of his inner man onto the warped and torn pages of his favorite blue journal. He wrote past the margin as if Mead had not created enough lines to contain his thoughts. Unconsciously mumbling future lines of poetry, rain fell on his window and with every strike of lightning, instead of thunder, the bone-chilling shrill of his mother's voice followed.

"Reefy! Reefy! Reef! "

Only his mother called him "Reefy" and it, accompanied with her intolerable tone, strummed the wrong chord of his nerves.

"Reefy! Come down here right now!"

Despite the orchestra of ultimate annoyance, the wheel of creativity continued to spin and began the uncontrollable spasms that he called handwriting. Not intimidated by structure, he wrote with an almost handicapped slant and skipped from the title of the page to the bottom.

> *Where is God? Is He betwixt the everything and nothingness where the son of darkened poetry refuses to shine? Or is He between the distant emptiness that rains from the clouds of my mind?*

"Reefy! Don't make me come up there!" she screamed, as if the threat of intrusion would defer her need to travel up the steps to Shareef's bedroom. "Reefy!"

Dead to the world, Shareef continued to write.

> *How can a concrete people be led by an intangible leader? Cupped as if waiting to detain fluid, I proclaimed, "In my hands, I now hold GOD." But with*

a clenched fist, the fight I must now resist because I realize that my hand holds nothing and the impalpable DOES NOT EXIST!!

With the final stroke of the pen, his door burst open. The petite and malnourished physique of Shareef's mother stood in the doorway. She smelled of baby spit, perfume and alcohol. She wore a painted face of impatient anger covering an arrogant smile of deceit. As her short hair hung as high as her mini skirt, she stood, arms folded and waited for attention. Shareef bowed his head toward his work and brainstormed his next literary adventure.

Ignoring the cold shoulder given in exchange for her shrieking charade, she snapped with an insolent tone. "Shareef Lamar Jones III," she said his full name whenever Shareef ignored her. This retort only led to him ignoring her even more because he was named after his father, but since his grandfather's name was Malachi that only made him Shareef Lamar Jones II. He never took the time to point this out to her.

"Shareef, I know you heard me yelling your name from downstairs. Are you deaf, dumb, or just my son? Do you hear me talking to you?" She gestured her hands to accompany her attitude. "Any way, your baby sister needs changing and she won't stop crying. I shouldn't have to come up here and make you handle your business."

"First of all, your babies are not my responsibility, and I shouldn't have to clean up after your mistakes." Shareef shot back as if he had a planned response to everything his mother had to say.

She attempted to conjure some emotion and pity, but failed miserably. "I got four kids and no husband and all I ask from you is a little help, Reefy."

With a heartless sigh, Shareef stood and stated under his breath, "That's not my problem." He scratched his left temple as he often did during times of distress. "Why don't you ask one of your boyfriends to do it?"

Cut to the bone by Shareef's attack on her wanton licentiousness, she carried on as if no harm had been done and it had all been a humorless joke. "Whatever. I'm about to go to the club so you need to watch your sisters."

"I can't watch them." Shareef mellowed to a less manly tone. "Tonight is the poetry slam and you know it. I have been mentioning it for weeks."

"Oh, you know I don't be listening to you boy. I don't know why you're so excited about this poetry stuff any way. 'Cause if I don't listen to you then you know ain't nobody else gon' listen to you, especially if they got to pay." She chuckled and then looked at herself in the mirror doing the Motorcycle dance. "I got to party while I'm still thirty years young. You can be boring with your poems while you watch your kid sisters." She walked to his desk, bent over and got in his face. "Maybe they can learn something." She walked out and left the house.

Shareef didn't expect to see her again until the next morning. He would not be surprised if he were to find her passed out in the yard on his way to school on Monday.

On most nights, Shareef stared out of his window and watched the sky dangle stars over the city streets of Portland, Oregon — his freedom from the pain. But tonight the stars hid from him, and the rain fell like tears that pride wouldn't let him shed. So he let his gaze fixate on the ceiling. His thoughts became grains of sand inside the glass walls of the mind, counting down the moments until he could share his message on stage.

I gotta go, Shareef thought as the last granule of sand ran out of his mind. He grabbed his journal and pen, put on his jacket and headed downstairs. Reciting his poem out loud, his steps down the stairs seemed to be in rhythm with his words.

"How am I supposed to express the hues of an empty canvas?" Step. "Then climb the tree that grew when faith was planted." Step. "I never actually saw anyone plant the seed." Step. "But I'm positive that it's there. It's gotta be."

As he reached the end of the narrow staircase studded with children's toys, his grandmother walked through the front door. Sunlight. Shareef crossed the desolate earth that was his living room to greet the sun after his storm. Before he reached her, she reminded him of his rain.

"Where is your mother?"

To avoid the discomfort of seeing his grandmother disappointed he muttered, "The club." He tried to elude an immanent speech about where she went wrong when raising his mother, and how he should be a good Christian young man and take care of his younger siblings. He loved his grandmother, but he hated her for her religion. She always tried to force it on him. He tried changing the subject, "So Granny, you sure are home early. Tell me something, did you come from work early just to see me?"

Her glare of disbelief burned right through Shareef's whimsical attempt at bringing humor to the situation. "The club? What do you mean she went to the club? Who's going to stay here and watch the babies?" She nodded toward the three innocent faces who sat cross legged at an unhealthy distance from the television. "Don't you have to go to that poetry slam that you've been talking about?" She gently touched his hands before he could answer. "It's okay. I'll watch them. You go ahead on and make your grandmamma proud."

Too appreciative for words, he kissed her on the forehead and then hugged her. Moments like these were common, but his love for her was bittersweet. He and his grandmother had their problems. His disdain for doctrine and dogma spread to her, as she shoved it down his throat. Sixty-one and nearing retirement, Shareef's grandmother put in long hours as a nurse in the local senior citizen's home. She paid rent, took care of her daughter and her daughter's children. He felt indebted to her, so for that reason he kept this hatred deep down under lock and key.

Embraced by the sun, the rose growing through the concrete realized that she was a double edged sword; both the source that allowed him to grow and the source that aided him in withering away. When he stepped out of the house he slowly closed the door. He heard his grandmother say, "I don't know where I went wrong raising that child. She don't act like no child of mine!"

The bus ride to the club reminded him of his sisters. As the rain ended, he pictured them smiling and basking in the sun even though the night sky shone moonlight over the horizon. Upon reaching his destination, Shareef headed to the back of the coffee house / jazz club — depending on what day you came — where he sat backstage alone. Well, not completely alone. He had his pen and pad and that was all he needed. His creativity flowed.

Poetry is the only thing that keeps me alive. Everything outside of it is constantly falling apart. My mother — the root of all evil — is living the childhood that I robbed her of. So I have to raise the branches stemming from the tree yet I am but a branch myself. My grandmother — a modern day Jesus — she sacrifices herself for us, but only to portray this

Christian super mother image. She really doesn't love me because she doesn't value my beliefs; or lack thereof. My father — I only know that he existed because of this one image of him leaving me, tattooed to my brain when I was small. My grandmother used to tell me that tattoos were a sin, maybe that's why I felt that I was so impure, so tainted, permanently scarred. Being foreign in my native land where can I go but to Poetry? I feel so caged in; no one wants to let me be free. So many alien thoughts invading planet Mind imprisoned is all that I can be. But then again what's the point of being free when others superimpose their cages on and around you? The same ones who love you are the same ones who tied you up and bound you, knotted their thoughts around you with the hopes that you would become them.

Marveled by the idea of freedom, Shareef stared off into nothingness.

"Sir. Sir. Sir!" A stern voice announced, "You're up next."

Shook by the sight of a man with a clipboard, Shareef drifted back to reality.

"Are you Shareef Jones?"

Shareef nodded and stretched.

"Well you're up next."

Shareef stood and collected his thoughts as he walked to the stage. It was like going home for him.

An eager crowd awaited as the mistress of ceremony gave renditions of her favorite Langston dreams, captivating their imaginations with reveries while they were yet awake. She gave them slow, low, melodic tones. They responded with explosions that lead to recoils of anticipation. Waiting behind

48

the purple curtains, Shareef's nerves were suspended in the sky where they became a lasso tied about his neck.

"Ladies and gentlemen, please give a warm welcome for our next poet... Shareef Jones! Come on up, Shareef."

The quiet before the storm, and then... eruptions. To calm his tensions, Shareef tried to think of sunlight, but the eruptions of the crowd blocked the sun with cloudless configurations of anxiety. The curtains inched open like a purple sea as if it were his veil removed. Shareef tried franticly to remember the patch work of the poem that he had written all day, but its entirety hid behind those configurations in his mind. Darkness fell. The eruptions intensified as if every voice in America joined in joyously, but when he looked into the soul of the crowd he only saw a sea of faces. Faces that resembled his grandmother, his mother, his father and his siblings. The crowd was his oppressor. Shareef took one more shot at remembering his poem, but it was too late. He had already relinquished himself unto the truth.

"Liberty bells ringing, uncracked. Liberty bells ringing around me. But the butt of the world's rifle has been shoved into my ideological stomach. They've tried to suffocate me with my own dreams But those liberty bells won't stop ringing... they won't... stop because I have relinquished myself unto truth."

The crowd sat silent as if they were trying to retrieve the anticipation that they had given earlier. That did not affect Shareef in the slightest bit. He bowed away as the curtains fell.

~ ~ ~ ~ ~ ~ ~

Shareef raised the blinds to let the sunrays raise his consciousness. He sat on the burgundy chaise lounge setting next to the large office window.

The doctor entered the room and took a seat behind the oversized oak desk. "Hello, Mr. Jones. I am Dr. Limburg and I will be assessing you. Tell me, what brings you here today?"

"I don't know. My grandmother says that I have issues with neglect or something like that." Shareef eyeballed the window next to him. "Do you mind if I open the window?"

Dr. Limburg nodded. Shareef stood and swung the window open to soak in the spring time equinox.

"Where was I," Shareef asked, as he stared out the window.

"You were telling me that your grandmother thought you should see a psychologist because of your feelings of neglect. Why would she think that you feel neglected?"

"Oh yeah, that's it." Shareef turned toward the long sofa. "Like I was saying, she sent me here to…"

Distracted by the window in the office, Shareef turned toward it once more. The intense sunlight reminded him of something, but he could not place a finger on it. The rays seemed to reach out for him, beckoning him to meet their grasp. He stared at the ceiling in deep thought and said, "Good bye." Shareef jumped out of the third story window and landed in a pile of freedom.

Saturday Pages
By Meta E. Lee

My most favorite thing that I own is a calendar. "You can't fit much of a day on that," Grandpa said. "It's no bigger than a folded dollar bill." He gave me a folded-up dollar to show me what he meant.

Every page is a whole day and it's all about mothers. It has poems about mothers and little stories about mothers. It tells how they love you...no matter what. Some of the mothers are famous. Some are really beautiful and wear fancy clothes. Other mothers are just regular moms like mine. When I got my calendar at Christmas, I drew bright rainbows on the Saturdays. The Saturday pages are better than all the other days combined.

When the Saturdays are over, I tear out that page. I draw a smiley face on the paper and sometimes a frown. Depends what happened. I hide my special pages in Grandpa's old wallet along with my folded-up dollar bill.

I woke up extra early on Saturday and put on my old blue dress.

"Young lady," Grandma said, "that dress is ready for the ragbag. It's too small for you. The buttons are about to pop off. Why don't you wear that red skirt? Or your pink shorts?"

"No, Grandma, this is Saturday and I'm going to wear my blue dress. It's kind of like Mom's dress."

"People will think that's all you have to wear. Your mother will worry that I don't buy you nice clothes."

"Grandma, this is Saturday and I'm going to wear my blue dress." Blue's the color of my mom's eyes. Blue's what my mom wears all the time.

Grandma looked like she was starting to cry. "Whatever you want, dear."

One day real soon Mom and I will get all dressed up. We'll have a party and eat lots of cookies and candy. We'll take turns reading my Saturday pages. Mom can wear whatever she wants. I bet she'll choose yellow. She says that yellow's a happy color because it reminds her of the sun. I'll wear my red skirt and a tee shirt with a fancy design. But for now, me and Mom wear blue. Blue's what my mom wears. My mom is in prison.

My Life
By William E. Campbell, Jr.

I grew up in the projects of Dayton, Ohio with my parents, three brothers and two sisters. My father, an alcoholic, argued or picked fights with my mom about little things. He accused her of messing around and when she left for work, he followed her to make sure that's where she went.

At fourteen, I hung around three guys who abused alcohol, pills and marijuana. I soon followed suit. Whatever they got involved in, I was down with it. I wanted to fit in and not be an outcast. Coming up in the 70s, I needed to be known as a boy who participated.

To support our drinking and marijuana habits, our four-man gang cased the community. We pinpointed unoccupied houses and apartments and then broke into them. I even stole from my family to appease my habit. I lifted antique ashtrays, boxed items like old-fashioned flower pots, lighters and fifty-cent pieces. My father accused my mother of siding with me and my siblings. He felt my mother let me steal from him, and that shifted his anger towards her. I never owned up to it. Perhaps that was one reason for my parents' divorce.

At age sixteen, and already two years behind, I dropped out of school. I joined the Job Corp in Wisconsin and completed a trade in interior and exterior decorating and painting. I obtained my GED and played league basketball. I received two offers: work as a painter in Corpus Christi, Texas or attend a small junior college outside Illinois on a basketball scholarship. I declined both. I missed turning up the bottle and rolling up joints. Nothing excited me more than going to the clubs and hanging out in the parks rolling dice or playing cards.

By December 1979, I was on my way back to Dayton. At twenty years old, I resided in a two-bedroom project apartment with my mother, sister and niece. My parents were separated and battling for custody of my youngest brother, Chris.

The apartment reeked of mildew like the stench in the basement of an abandoned house that had flooded several times. When the lights were turned on, little creatures scattered and ran inside the cracks in the walls like a herd of buffalo galloping across a field. The windows and sills looked like an un-defrosted freezer caked with thick ice. Cold air blew through the vents and puffs of smoke drifted from my mouth when I breathed.

Three months later, I signed up for the Army. Jobs were scarce and I needed to be independent to help my mom. I got a ride to Cincinnati, took my physical and swore in. The next day I was at Fort Knox, Kentucky Army Base for basic training and schooling.

My abuse of alcohol continued and intensified. Everyday at 4:00 pm I raced to the bar for a pitcher of draft beer. I drank until my last dollar was gone and then stumbled back to my unit. As my obsession worsened, I neglected my duties as a soldier. On several occasions, I packed some clothes and went absent without leave (AWOL) for ten to thirty days at a time. Insubordinate.

When I did report for duty, I followed the same routine: go to the post exchange (P. X.) to grab some beer and a sandwich. One day as I sat outside the P. X., enjoying the clear blue skies and absorbing the hot steamy sun, a soldier from my unit approached me. His form of play aggravated me on a regular basis. I was well juiced when he staggered up to me.

"Wh-what you doing," he said, with his finger pointed in my face. "What k-k-kinda sandwich you got?"

"Man, go on somewhere and leave me alone."

"I-I-I said, 'What you eatin'?'" He lost his balance and knocked over my beer.

"I need you to move away from me."

"You n-need me to what?" He moved toward me and raised his voice. "You don't tell me what to do." With his last word, he shot a glob of spit that hit me in the face.

I stood, swung my portable boom box and struck him across the head. Two first lieutenants in the area tried to break up the fight. By the time the bout was over, I was charged with assault on the officers and locked in the stockade for ten days. The judge ordered me to appear in court in two weeks.

Fear ripped through me, so I packed my AWOL clothes and went back to live with my mom and sister.

"How did you manage to get home again so soon," my mother asked as she wiped her hands on her apron. "You were just here last month."

"I got an extra thirty days of leave." Although I had several reasons for defying Uncle Sam's house rules, my female bed partner was the main one. Several months later, the Army stopped my financial allotment, so I stopped giving money to my mother.

With her finger in my face, my mother said, "You better get back to the Army before the military police (M. P.) come looking for you."

I continued to drink, party and run the streets. I found ways to feed my alcoholic thirst; hustled, donated blood, stole or leeched off of others. I picked a fight with one of my closest friends and threatened to beat up another. That guy came to my mother's house and fired a rifle into the star-lit sky.

"That's it. You have got to get out of my house." My mother grabbed my clothes, packed them in a suitcase and drove me to the Greyhound Bus Station. "Here," she tossed a piece of paper at me. "Take this one-way ticket to Fort Knox and handle your business."

When I arrived at the base, I turned myself in at the M. P. station. "I'm a tenth-cavalry scout returning from AWOL."

They took me into custody and by April 1981, I received my papers for a dishonorable discharge. I had served thirteen months of a three-year enlistment, and for more than half of that time, I was AWOL.

What am I going to do now? Stuck in Kentucky, 200 miles from Dayton and without money to get home, I walked out of the front entrance of the base. The scorching sun beamed down on my t-shirt-covered back and bare face.

I hitched a ride here and there, but none lasted for more than fifteen miles. I walked back roads and down the highway while thousands of vehicles blew past me. My callused feet throbbed and ached. Each step felt like drudging on hot coals. At every off ramp, I exited the highway in search of comfort and water.

Buckets of pouring rain and winds as strong as Dorothy's Kansas tornado filled the second night of my journey. Hawkeye vision couldn't pierce through the dark skies. I sought shelter at a gas station and camped outside the restroom. The stench of urine rushed into my nostrils as the fear of racism filled my mind — a black man alone in the back roads of southern hatred. The rainstorm ensued until seven the next morning. My journey home continued.

On the third day of my pilgrimage, I reached the off ramp to my mother's apartment. I released an extended sigh and wiped the sweat from my forehead. The University of Dayton Arena never looked so inviting.

I arrived at the empty apartment about three that afternoon. I borrowed food and drinks and tucked them in my backpack.

The next day I swiped several slices of ham. I knew my family's schedule and only returned to the apartment when no one was home.

Several days passed before the disappearing pork and dwindling orange juice signaled to my mother that I had been in the apartment. She left a note on the refrigerator.

Wait for me to get home.

Mom

When she arrived home from work, she grilled me. "I cannot believe that you have been kicked out of the Army." She plopped her purse on the kitchen table. "You could have gone to college on a basketball scholarship or went to Texas to work." She walked to the refrigerator and grabbed the plate of ham scraps.

Slouched in the chair with my head drooped, I sat silent.

"You need to find a job and you have exactly one month to do so. You've had plenty of opportunities to live a life of comfort," she slid the plate across the table toward me. "But you chose chaos, drugs and alcohol." She walked out of the kitchen.

My shortcomings and follies caught up with me and in 1982, I was convicted of a felony. I served thirteen months of an eighteen-month sentence. The eight-by-ten efficiency unit came complete with a personal latrine and urine-polluted air. My nightly lullaby was a medley of rocks that slammed against concrete walls to distract rodents. Inside a rusted cage, I felt like a trapped animal. My every movement required permission from the overseer. The prison wake up call caused me to flash back to my three-day journey from Kentucky.

"I'm sick of me. Today I choose to turn my life around." I flushed the toilet and watched a roach swirl away. "I will never see the inside of a cage again."

Valerie L. Coleman

Upon release in July 1983, I didn't have a place to stay. My father gave me another chance and allowed me to live with him provided I find employment. I held down several jobs before I found a new drug of choice; crack cocaine. In 1989, I met an attractive light-skinned woman who introduced me to enhanced herbs rolled in cigarette paper. Pre-moes contain marijuana and crack cocaine, while ciga-moes have cigarette tobacco and crack cocaine. Both "cigarettes" led me to pipe smoking.

The ongoing dependency left me with short-term memory loss. On one occasion, someone stole the gym shoes off my feet while I slept in a neighbor's front yard. Another time, after a night of drunken partying with a couple of buddies, I almost stomped a man to death.

"That's it! I'm not drinking anymore!" I'd quit drinking for a week or two and then settle back to the same routine. My addiction to crack cocaine and alcohol landed me in prison again.

I am now serving a twenty-eight-to-sixty-five-year prison sentence. I have been incarcerated since June 15, 1991 and free of alcohol and drugs for over fifteen years. Although incarceration has limited my accessibility to substances, my being clean is largely due to me taking a stand. Drugs and alcohol are readily available in correctional facilities. Opportunities to get high have been presented to me too many times to count. But when I look back at how alcohol and drugs damaged my life, I push away from the temptation.

Drinking, drugging, running the streets and hanging around alcoholics kept me dormant. It took a prison sentence to make me realize that I needed to change. Transformation. Not because it was in my best interest, but because I wanted to progress in life; survive in life.

Life is much more than a bottle of beer, pulling on a pipe or puffing a joint. Life is about sacrifice, family, culture and self-awareness. Therefore, I have made a choice to better myself. I have been attending Alcoholics Anonymous meetings for over two years and will continue to attend upon my release from prison. I have obtained an associates degree in human services and I encourage guys who are being released back into society. I advise them to stay away from the things that kept their lives dormant.

We all have opportunities in life. We all have a gift from God. But are we willing to sacrifice the other things to pursue our dreams or goals? We'd rather sell drugs or abuse ourselves than pursue our opportunities.

I know that being black poses a unique problem of social, psychological, or even physical survival. Whenever I saw another black person getting stopped by the police, I wondered how race figured into it. When I used to go to the store and the salespeople gave me an extra bit of scrutiny, I pondered. Whenever whites are accommodated more than blacks in prison, my first thought is race. Little things like that remind me that we may be paying a black tax — "psych tax."

We must educate ourselves politically, socially and economically to avoid the enslavement of correctional facilities. Stay focused in school. Learn and apply the taught principles particularly history and global awareness. When you know, you can grow. When you grow, you can go.

Do you want to go anywhere? Don't make the mistakes I made. Grab your opportunities when they come. The lifestyle you choose determines your destiny.

Traits of a Man
By Red Handed

I wasn't raised in a devout Christian household, but rather a house full of sin and wickedness. My mom, however, made my sister and I go to church and get on our knees every night to recite the model prayer in Matthew 6:9-15.

The thirteenth verse haunted my thoughts. "Do not bring us into temptation but deliver us from the wicked one." At six years old, I often wondered about "the wicked one." Was he the boogieman? Was he one of my uncles? Was he an actor in a movie? Curiosity got the best of me, so I searched for this wicked one. I wanted to find him and ask him why my mother wanted me to be delivered from him. Was he really so bad that we couldn't be friends and play together?

I lived with my mom, sister, grandparents, Aunt Terry and Uncle Ken. My grandparents and mother worked while the rest of us went to school. Since Grandma worked nights, I was forced to go to a babysitter.

"Red, Mommy has to work to put clean clothes on your back and food in your mouth," Mom said, as she prepared for work. "And since your deadbeat daddy ain't around, we're going to have to send you to a babysitter."

"I don't want to go. Want to stay wit Grandma."

With her hands on her hips, Mom said, "Well you don't have a choice. You're going!"

I hit the floor and threw a temper tantrum; cried, flailed my arms and stomped my feet like tomorrow would never come. On most days, this routine worked and I'd get my way. After all, I was the baby of the house. But on this day, Mom wasn't going for it. She grabbed my ear and dragged me down the street to the babysitter's house. That's the day I met Anger, Pride and Hate. I was also introduced to The Wicked One who soon became my best friend. In no time at all, I picked up his traits.

The babysitter was an old German lady with a heavy accent. She had long, grayish-brown hair and a pair of small-rimmed glasses that hung slightly off her big nose. At first appearance, she seemed mean and I didn't like her. I found out real quick that she didn't like to play.

We spent most of our time in the dimly lit basement. I felt like a prisoner waiting for parole. I sat on the floor and ate cold bologna, chips and oatmeal pies and then washed it down with ice cold milk. She sat in a burgundy leather recliner, watched soaps and expected me to take a nap and be quiet. She would've had an easier time getting Paris Hilton out of a shopping mall than getting me to go to sleep. She grew tired of our Tom and Jerry dance, so she decided to give in and play Hide and Seek with me. She sat in the chair and closed her eyes. I tied a scarf around her face and bound her hands with a jump rope. As she counted to twenty, I went up the steps, out the door and up the street to Grandma's house.

I curled up under Grandma who was in a peaceful sleep. When the phone rang, I got scared. I had a feeling it was Mom. Grandma rolled over after the fourth ring and answered with much attitude.

"Hello!"

My mom's voice was so loud I heard her say, "Red left the sitter. Is he there?" I tugged at Grandma's leg and shook my head.

Grandma looked down at me and said, "Yes, he's right here, so stop worrying."

Mom's voice raised several more octaves. "I don't have time for this nonsense! I'm trying to work. Send him back and I'll deal with his butt when I get home!"

"He doesn't like it down there," Grandma said smiling at me. "He's spending the rest of the day here with me and you betta not whoop him!" She ended the call.

Grandma was my savior and I knew I could get away with anything.

~ ~ ~ ~ ~ ~ ~

The Wicked One and I were tighter than turtlenecks in the wintertime. The older I got the more I allowed him to influence my decisions.

I didn't care much for school. It probably had to do with the fact that I was chubby and the butt of everyone's fat jokes. I didn't like to be laughed at or humiliated, hence came Pride and Self-consciousness. At first I didn't think it bothered me because I stayed quiet and internalized it. All smiles on the outside, but filled with anger and destructive thoughts on the inside. That's when I met another good friend; her name, Depression. My boy, The Wicked One, sensed my pain. He told me that he had a plan to get me the much needed love and attention that I lacked. I took his advice and launched Plan Get Attention.

One Saturday afternoon, bored with my toys and tired of being in the house, I went into the backyard. My dude, Jay, wasn't around so I created some excitement. I smuggled five strike-anywhere matches that came inside a blue wooden box from the kitchen drawer and headed straight for the green shed. I grabbed the tan wool blanket that covered the lawnmower and struck the match on the ground.

WHOOSH! The blanket went up in flames that spread fast. Scared, I grabbed the red and yellow canister and poured what

I thought was water on the fire. The flames rose like the sun in the morning. My nosey Uncle Ken smelled the smoke and ran out the house.

"What are you doing, you fat idiot? Trying to burn down the house?" He shoved me out the way. I stood in shock and watched the flames rise. Uncle Ken shook his head, mumbled some profanities and then grabbed the hose. He put out the fire. I ran inside the house, jumped in my bed and pretended to be asleep. That trick didn't work. A soon as my mom found out, she snatched me out the bed and lit up my butt with a thick, black leather belt. Grandma couldn't save me from that one, actually she whooped me too.

Momma warned on more than one occasion, "Boy, we going to beat the wickedness out of you or else!"

Those whoopings were the first of many. I enjoyed the attention and the beat downs only made me stronger. I continued to mess up. I took candy and toys from the neighborhood convenience store. I'd been doing it for so long that I figured I could keep getting away with it.

All good things must come to an end. That's exactly what happened when Grandma took me and my Aunt Harrah to the bank. After Aunt Harrah cashed her check, she stuck the bills, a bunch of twenties inside a little bank envelope, in her purse. She set her purse on the floor in the backseat with me.

That's a lot of candy and toy money. I'd be the envy of all the kids in the neighborhood. I thought as I took two twenty-dollar bills. *She won't miss it.*

She missed it. Grandma questioned me like a detective trying to solve a murder case. "Red, Aunt Harrah is missing forty dollars. Did you see it fall out of her purse?"

I shook my head. Grandma always knew when I was lying, so she took my reply as a sign of guilt.

Later that day, she found the money under my pillow and tore my butt up something fierce. After she got done, my mom continued the whooping. I got whooped for over twenty minutes and was sore for a week.

My quest for attention had not made me happy at all. I became numb to the pain of the whoopings and verbal attacks I received at school and from my uncle. The anger inside of me grew. I didn't know how to express myself verbally, so I did it physically. I did what I knew best — fight. I picked fights with people for no reason and had a fly mouth. It didn't take long for it to catch up with me. The neighborhood bullies cornered me behind some bushes and beat me with baseball bats. I didn't cry. I took it like a soldier because I knew that revenge would be mine.

~ ~ ~ ~ ~ ~ ~

The traits I developed as a kid carried into adulthood. I solved most of my problems with violence. It worked for me as a kid, so why wouldn't it work as an adult? I hung onto Anger, Pride, and Depression which kept The Wicked One and me tight like O. J.'s gloves.

Hopeful that I'd change my ways, Mom sent me to California. I lived with my Uncle Marvin for a couple of years. I spun cuts as a DJ and produced beats for local aspiring Rap/R&B artists. I experienced a great deal of success, had relations with lots of females and made nice money. But the biggest transformation came when I moved back to Ohio. Gone was the chubby, timid kid whose bark was worse than his bite. I was a new man physically and mentally, but my emotional state was still messy. I lived for money, music and girls.

On September 13, 1995, three months before my twenty-third birthday, my life changed. I'd been with a beautiful caramel-complected chick sure to be Mrs. Red Handed.

For most of our turbulent four years, we fought like championship fighters to stay together. Tiara was by far the baddest chick I'd ever dated. Raised in the church, she was a good girl, but I corrupted her. I turned her out on sex, money and living the "good life."

Over time, I grew tired of feuding with her family. They felt that I wasn't good enough for her, so I ended the relationship. Bitter about the break-up, Tiara had the thugs of her family rob and beat me. I put in work and gave as good as I got, but being outnumbered and outgunned, it was a fight that I couldn't win. I got it handed to me and couldn't accept how I got beat down. Even as a kid, the batting bullies didn't get me that bad. My longtime friend, Pride, would not allow Tiara's thugs to get the best of me.

While I healed, my old flame, Depression, came back with her friend, Alcohol, and together we formulated a plan for revenge. Since Tiara liked setting people up, I was determined to force her hand, but this time I would be ready. I was going to hold her hostage and make her call her family to save her. When they arrived, I was going to blast them like a scene from *Menace II Society*. As tough as I thought I was, I didn't have the heart for murder. With that plan out the window, I devised something less violent.

I stopped at the corner store where Depression and I picked up her girl, Alcohol. I held Alcohol tight and became intoxicated with her kiss. I drove to Tiara's job to give her a chance to come clean about the set-up.

Just as I pulled up, Tiara stepped out of her car. I parked and then walked up on her. "Tiara, wassup? I need to holler at you a minute."

She looked at me and then rolled her eyes. "Not right now. I'm looking for my keys."

I reached into the back pocket of my jeans and pulled out a black semi-automatic. "Oh, you're gonna to talk!"

Fear leaped into her doe-like brown eyes. She complied and walked with me toward my car. Just as we got a couple of feet from the car, she took off running.

"Stop! I just need to talk!" Tiara ran toward the building. My boy, The Wicked One, Pride and Anger pumped me up like a Reebok pump. *We know you aren't going to let her play you like that! She already played you once.* I popped off two shots in the air.

She fell to the ground. My legs trembled at the thought that I may have killed her by accident. One of her co-workers came outside and helped her in the building. Thank God. I went inside to make sure she was okay but failed to find her. I left.

Four hours later, a bunch of police kicked in my door with guns drawn and arrested me. I was charged with a boatload of felonies; attempted murder, two felonious assaults, kidnapping, burglary and two weapons charges.

As soon as I got to the County Jail, I called on God and recited the model prayer. "Lord, please deliver me from The Wicked One."

After twelve years of incarceration, I realize that I was The Wicked One in my thoughts and actions. In a sense, I asked God to deliver me from myself and the traits I held onto from childhood.

Now that I have God in my life, I no longer hear from my old friends, The Wicked One, Depression, Anger, Pride and Alcohol.

A Pilferer and Habitual Liar
By Charles E. Loper, III

Pilferer: A petty thief
Habitual liar: One who constantly lies, no matter the situation.

Cel woke up on a soggy mattress and glanced around his cluttered bedroom. When he noticed his mom hadn't washed his clothes the night before, he slipped out of the bed and ventured into his tomboyish sister's room. Filch! Cel exited her room, showered, dressed and left for school.

Later that night, Cel relaxed in his bedroom when his sister arrived home from work. She burst into his room and looked around. "Did you take my new Gap jeans out my dresser?"

"No, I would never take anything out of your room," Cel said, as he raised his right hand. "I swear to God."

She cocked her head to the right, rolled her eyes and then spun around. She stormed into her room and slammed the door. *She must have believed me,* Cel thought, as he shut his door. He folded the jeans he wore to school and hid them under his mattress.

~ ~ ~ ~ ~ ~ ~

Two years later, Cel, now at the legal driving age, hung out with some friends at the end of his street. In an area called "The Fields," they watched the more fortunate kids ride motor-powered dirt bikes across the grassy pasture. On his way home, he noticed a slightly used motorbike in a neighbor's back yard. A "For Sale" sign was propped on the handlebars. Excited, Cel rushed home. He found his mother in the living room watching TV.

"Mom, I saw a dirt bike that only cost $300!" He slapped his hands to emphasize each word. "Can I get it for Christmas?"

She looked up from the television. "Son, you know I can't afford that."

With his hopes of riding in the meadows swirling down the drain, he turned on his heel and headed for the steps.

"Hold on, Cel. Call your dad and see if he'll go half with me."

A smile spread across Cel's face. He rushed in the kitchen and dialed his dad's number.

"Hello."

"Dad, Mom told me to ask if you would go half on a motorbike for me. It only cost $300."

"I don't know, son." He paused and then sighed. "Where would you ride it?"

"In the fields down the street."

"Maybe next year. I don't want you to get hurt."

Cel hung up the phone and locked himself in his room for the rest of the night. A few nights later, he snuck out the house and met some friends. Within thirty minutes, they were back in their beds.

Early the next morning, Cel was awakened by a loud knock. His mother opened the front door and was greeted by a police officer.

"Can I help you?"

The officer removed his hat and nodded. "Yes ma'am. We're looking for your son. We found his fingerprints on a retrieved stolen motorbike."

"He's not here," she said, as she pulled the door close to her body. "But I know you got the wrong child."

"Well, we need to speak with him anyway. We'll be back later."

She shut the door and ran up the steps. "Boy, whose stuff did you steal?"

Cel wiped his eyes, as he sat up in bed. "What are you talking about Mom? I didn't steal nothing. I swear to God." He plopped back on his bed.

She squinted her eyes and tightened her lips. "You better not be lying to me or I'm going to ship you off to your father."

Cel knew there was no chance of that. And besides, his mother believed him.

~ ~ ~ ~ ~ ~ ~

April 1995, tired and fed up with his lies and deceit, Cel's mother sent him to live with his father.

On his way out of his father's house, Cel came across something valuable lying on the kitchen table. Filch! He went off to school like any other day.

Cel sat on his bed doing homework later that evening when his father entered. "Son, did you accidentally pick my pager up from the kitchen table this morning?"

"No, Dad. I swear to God I didn't pick it up."

His father shook his head and then exited the room.

Two weeks later, Cel was home alone when he received an unexpected visit from a much older and very attractive neighborhood girl. He invited her in and escorted her back to his room. Afterwards, she gave him a kiss and then searched through her purse. "Can I use your restroom?"

"Go ahead." Cel watched her leave the room. His stare then diverted to the purse she tossed on the couch. The temptation to rifle through it consumed him, but the love she showed him wouldn't allow his hands to react to the urges. He escorted her out the house, returned to his room and daydreamed about his experience for a few hours.

Five minutes after his dad came home from work, someone knocked on the door.

"Cel, come here!" His father yelled up the stairs.

Cel bounded down the stairs prepared to tell his friends that he was in for the night. His eyes widened when he saw the subject of his daydream sitting across from his dad in deep conversation. "What are you doing here?"

"Son, sit down," his father said and then patted the couch. "This young lady said that you had her over here earlier and stole $100 from her purse. I don't even want to know why you had her in here. I just need to know where her money is."

Confusion spread across Cel's face. *Is my habit that bad that I don't remember going in her purse,* he pondered. "I didn't take nothing from that girl." He furrowed his eyebrows and shrugged. "She's lying."

"There's only one thing I can do." His father reached in his wallet, pulled out five crispy twenty-dollar bills, and handed them to the girl.

"Don't give her nothing!" Cel stood, looked at his father and pointed at his accuser. "I didn't take her money. She's lying, Dad!" He directed his teary eyes on the girl. "Why are you doing this?" She gazed back at him, expressionless.

"You invited her over while I wasn't home. You put me in this position, now I've got to pay for your mistake." His father's attention turned to the girl. "Young lady, if I'm not here, do not come in my house."

"I won't and I'm sorry it came to this." She stuffed the money in her pocket and then left.

Cel sat alone on the couch with wet cheeks. He wondered why the girl lied on him and most of all, why his father believed her over him. Deep in his heart, he knew the reason, but it was yet to become known.

~ ~ ~ ~ ~ ~ ~

Over the years, the lies and deceptions that flowed from Cel's lips landed him in prison. Inspired by a friend, he decided to attend a Sunday morning church service. Tears streamed from his eyes, as the words of the jailhouse preacher pierced his heart.

"Life brings many challenges," the preacher said with the Bible clutched in his hands. "Trying to take the easy way out put us all in here. The devil makes it easy to lie, but the Lord helps us with the truth. Your lies will entrap you, but the truth will make you free."

All through the night, Cel tossed and turned in his bed. Compelled to get up, he crawled out of bed, dropped to his knees and prayed for forgiveness.

"Lord, forgive me for the life I've led." He sought the Lord for over an hour. Once finished, he sat at his desk and wrote apology letters to his family.

The first was to his sister, whom he robbed of many garments she worked so hard to buy. "Even though I had nothing, I had no right to take what was yours." The second letter was to his mom. He needed to purge the guilt he felt for bringing the police to her house on many occasions. "You didn't deserve the stress I caused." The final letter was to his father, who took him in, no matter his flaws. "I apologize for taking many things from the house that didn't belong to me. As God as my witness, I didn't take that girl's money, but I understand why I was an easy victim of her deceit."

~ ~ ~ ~ ~ ~ ~

Children learn to lie at a young age. Parents must teach their children to be truthful because if the cycle is not broken, the child could end up dead or in prison. If this story hits close to home, look back on your life, ask the Lord for forgiveness, and live a righteous life. Be truthful to yourself and others.

To Each His Own
By LaMont "B.I.G. Fridge" Needum

A path to enlightenment isn't necessarily a ray of light that shines down from Heaven and makes the soul dance. No, not for Fat Daddy. No hand touched me, no spiritual revelation — just calm.

I hadn't had a moment's peace since I took the hand of the devil in the summer of '88, the year I sold my first rock. I'm from a place called Short North, in Columbus, Ohio. We turned the Short North into a savage garden. No rival dealers were allowed. Period! The decision wasn't totally financial; it had more to do with tenacity. We were all like family, so it was decided that the residents of the Short would not be afraid to go outside their home at any time. For example, old folks would not be scared to go to the corner store to play numbers. We're from the old school of thought; we don't disrespect old folks or mess over children. We protected our own.

In the process, I lost my soul to the game. Money, sex, herb and hard liquor became my vices. And since black men are virtually powerless, the small increment of cogency I enjoyed was bliss.

They say that the wages of sin is death, but what is the price when you've already embraced your demise? I used to tell my lady that I wouldn't live to be twenty-three. Thank God I was wrong.

Some folks say that they believe in the Lord. The only time I actually acknowledged Him was in a hail of bullets and gun smoke, or when the grim one floated around us. Outside that, acknowledging God was merely a formality. Most folks won't admit that though.

The only reason I'm still breathing is due to the birth of my son. July 12, 1993, I got my first true confirmation of the Lord's existence. If there is such a thing as the Holy Ghost, I felt it the moment I set eyes on him. No vice can then or now compare to the euphoria that washed over me. His arrival slowed me down a bit, but it was still on in a major way. A year flew by and before I knew it, I was in a white man's cage serving two years for a petty drug trafficking charge. In the State joint, people either got better or slicker. I turned into a can of oil, or so I thought.

March 1995, eight months before my release, a homie passed me to the Columbus Dispatch. Uncle Sam had raided my turf and I was on the indictment. The sentence: forty-six years and nine months. I got a year for myself and one for all my co-defendants in what was the biggest gang conspiracy in Columbus' history. The gig was up. None of us really cared. Growing up in the projects was like growing up in prison. All my dudes were in with me so it was like my high school reunion on steroids. Not until I almost caught another case in the joint did life present itself in a different manner.

In 1997, a guy forced my hand and I beat him within an inch of his life. The Feds contemplated charges that could've gotten me an additional fifteen years. Locked in the equivalent of a broom closet with a toilet almost drove me insane. And trust me, the hole has driven many men mad. People say what they can and cannot do all the time, but sitting in a cell, with only you and your demons requires strength. The time alone forced me to observe the hate I had promulgated and concealed. My feelings ranged from anger to contrition. No more self medication, or getting high, to help me sweep the evil under the rug. For the first time, I got to know myself — come to find out, I'm not so bad after all.

April 1999, two days before my birthday, I received a precious gift. The Dispatch announced that we had won our appeal. We all knew the conspiracy was pretty much a stunt. Shoot, three months grinding it out in trial proved that. The sun shined down on the fat man again, at least for a while. Two weeks later, the Feds called in a favor from the State and had them drop an indictment on me. Vindictive prosecution. If a prosecutor is going to press charges, he isn't supposed to wait to see if you're going to win the appeal five years later. He's supposed to come with it in the interest of justice. These and many other rules about justice, freedom and the Amerikkkan way don't apply to black folks. Just ask the young groom from New York. May he rest in peace.

So, I'm back in F.C.C.C. and the Feds are making it as uncomfortable as possible. But I'm much tougher than hard times. Conspiracy was the key to dragging me into Federal Court, so I'm thinking new trial. Nope! The good ol' boys didn't grant a new trial, they simply found a way to turn WORDS into DRUGS (honest truth – it's called relevant conduct) and re-sentenced me to twenty-seven years. Life or forty-six calendars; few men will do all that time; but twenty-seven years in a Federal joint is a sentence that guys max out regularly. No parole. I'm through! And now I have to fight an additional fifteen to twenty-five years with the State. My body betrayed me and I fell sick. I never had the flu before, so I thought it was a high-powered cold. It almost took me out.

I braved the flu without medication. You never know how alone you are until you get sick in prison. No love. The brothers try to look out for you as best they can, but the unwritten rules of prison are designed for you to suffer alone and in silence. Men don't touch one another. Men don't make each other soup. And in the County Jail, where men come and go, no one cares if you live or die. In the penitentiary, we care for one another a little better because nothing changes. When someone dies in the pen, it reminds you of your own mortality.

The only real solace I found was in my mother's voice. No one and nothing compares to mother. Nothing! Big Rube sounded troubled when she answered the phone.

"You need to call Nell," she said.

"What's wrong?"

"Just call Nell."

Nell is short for Dannell, my oldest son's mother. Still sick, I struggled to stand and walk to the payphone. It took about three phone calls to get my girl to admit her major malfunction.

"Fridge," she said in a soft, quiet voice. "I got... I can't say it!" She didn't have to. Her admission caused my illness to subside temporarily. This woman gave me a reason to live by having my first child. On God's chessboard, I am a natural protector. When I fail to protect what I love, shame overtakes me. There was so much pressure on me — not that I cared about my own happiness, Nell and I weren't even together anymore. It's just...I viewed my girl as family. I'd already lost my Uncle Toney to A.I.D.S. Lost my home girl to it not long before, and now it was at my doorstep. I consoled her as best I could.

"It's gonna be okay, baby girl," I said as I cleared my throat and fought to stand up straight. "I need you to come visit me so we can make some plans. Things aren't gonna be easy, but I'm gonna help you through this."

"You promise?"

"I promise." Having firsthand knowledge of what H.I.V./A.I.D.S. did to my uncle; I took responsibility of keeping Nell's focus off of what she considered the inevitable. All of us are on the clock, no doubt, but once a person is diagnosed and their clock is set, well, that's a whole different animal.

My world was rocked. What was to happen to my son and stepdaughter if Nell didn't make it? How was I going to be able to do twenty-seven years plus the ten to twenty-five that the State was going to give me? Was I going to survive this flu? I hit a brick wall.

I talked to Nell until my body could no longer stand it. I returned to the crude metal and concrete dwelling. I hung my blanket over the bars, collapsed on the floor and did what I didn't do when the FBI took my entire youth from me. I did what I didn't do when my cousin, Jason, got killed in a car accident. I did what I didn't do when they found my homie, Cecil, dead in the trunk of a car. I could go on like that for hours, but what I did was cry.

Now mind you, I weigh between 290 to 410 pounds depending on if I'm working out or depressed. At six-foot-four and with a top-billing reputation in the streets and the joint, crying is *not* an option! But I did. The tears flowed like the Nile River and I didn't care who heard me. I was never going to kick it with Nell again. May never play ball with my sons. But the worst part was the powerlessness. Had Uncle Sam finally won? Was this going to be my last night on earth? Hot and cold flashes, full-body muscle ache, dehydration. I was going to die in a puddle of my own fluids on the floor of the Columbus County Jail; an unfitting death for a gangsta.

"Oh, God! Why is my luck so bad? Am I going to die like this? Why are You picking on me?" I knew why. He wasn't picking on me, it was just my turn. "What do You want from me?" I asked many questions that night, but one thing I didn't ask for was forgiveness. I'd made my bed and I intended to lay in it. Forgiveness is for the guilty, not the misled. "I turn it over to You." My last words before I blacked out.

~ ~ ~ ~ ~ ~ ~

I did not die. The violent shaking of my body woke me. I lay on the freezing concrete sicker than the day before. I crawled onto the metal slab, put on a blanket and then the hot flashes came. I got on the floor; cold flashes. Couldn't breathe, couldn't eat, but I made it through the night. The next day my trek home began. Like I said before; no light, no hand of God, no glorious revelation. God had given me all that I needed to survive; a strong immune system and an even stronger will.

I limped to the mirror. I was a mess, but I managed a smile. I had survived my darkest night. I hate to admit it, but if I didn't wake up the next morning, I would not have complained. That's just plain weak! It was not over for me. The test had been set and I didn't tap out. The words I spoke before I passed out were my declaration of faith. "In the beginning was the Word..." I know what that means now. I've learned to accept my blessings when they come instead of rejecting them.

Since then I've had my ups and downs, but the worst part is over. Nell left us not long ago and we're making it through that. Not everyone's story has a happy ending, but mine is filled with promise. Still don't have a religion — I don't like the politics — but I know God is real, and He truly does provide.

People ask me if I could do it all over again, what would I do different. I tell them, "Nothing." Of course, they think I'm crazy, but I figure why bother with wishful thinking? Life is about gains and losses; losses in life and love. To me, it's about what you do in the moments that you gain. Do you fully express your love? Do you do what you do with all the passion you can muster? Life and football are about inches and yards.

Sometimes you lose yardage, like I have; sometimes you gain yardage, like I have. But I refuse to bathe in regret because this is my story. It's not supposed to be like yours or anyone else's. It's mine, and I know that once a man gets out of his own way, he can accomplish what he wills. At least some of the time...

I'm still in prison, that hasn't changed. I'm still not happy, and I'm not supposed to be because prison absolutely sucks! But God has cleared the path for me and I'm walking it. For men like me, all that's needed is a little divine understanding to get out of our own way. God does work in mysterious ways, but the important part is that He **works**.

I sound a bit abrasive, I know. My environment requires it, and who knows, I might not be able to function in society after all of this. I've been gone for about thirteen years. But I've learned through that time in the County, as well as several other situations, that a man ain't a man until he realizes the world **ain't** about him! So get over yourself! I did. And that is certainly a gift from God.

Deception

By Brian Revere

With an extended smoker's cough, the old fragile man laughed. "I see they got you good," he said, as a herd of crooked corrections officers opened the door to my new home — my residence for the final seventeen months of my prison bid.

They tossed me on the cold, dusty floor and my head just missed the base of the toilet. I swiped the dust from my pants and then stood face-to-face with the great urban legend, Ol' Man Willie, a household name in the Ohio Prison System.

"Yeah, they beat you like a run away slave," Willie said, as he helped me to the top bunk. The aroma of cheap coffee and Marlboro enveloped his words.

Pain overtook me. Not from the blows of the closed fists and wooden sticks, but because I didn't spit in C.O. Lumscull's face for calling my mother out of her Christian name.

"Here, smoke this, Youngsta."

As I accepted his token of endearment, "Good lookin'" crept from my lips. A cloud of smoke engulfed me and I zoned off into a world outside the walls and razor fences.

Over the next few months, we formed a mutual tone of respect. I invested most of my days chasing a dollar, so we didn't have much common ground to build on. Some nights, we played a few games of chess when nothing was on television, but that's about it.

On December 13, Officer Lumscull worked the block on first shift. I remember the day because it was my daughter's eleventh birthday. I hadn't seen her since my second week in jail, over seven years. Earlier that week, I received word from my sister, Brandi, that she was given permission to bring my little girl to visit me.

At 12:30 pm, the phones rang to release guys waiting for visitors. At least a thousand times, the bells chimed and at least a thousand times my heart raced with anticipation. A long list of names were called; all but one, mine. Lost in a pool of rage, I paced as every passing minute drew closer to the 2:30 pm cut-off time.

"This isn't like Brandi," I said, as I tightened my fists. Crazy thoughts swam around in my mind. I walked up to Officer Lumscull. As usual, he was leaned back in his chair with his feet perched on the edge of the old desk and his hands clasped behind his head. "C.O., can you call Operations to see if there was a visit for Thomas?"

With his upper lip curled, he grimaced. "If I haven't called your name, then the answer is no. Now go somewhere and get out of my face!"

Devastated, I returned to my cell. Hoping to bring a quick end to the day, I slept.

A couple of hours later, close to the four o'clock count, Willie strolled into the cell. His cough-obstructed whistling woke me. I snatched the pillow from under my head and covered my face with it.

"Here you go, Youngsta." He tossed a Butterfinger candy bar on my bed.

I sat up to see what hit my leg. *Are you kidding me? Even this old fool got a visit today?* The rage and curiosity inside me grew.

"There was a nice looking lady up there today," he said as he lit up a smoke. "She had a little girl with her too. They sat up there the whole two hours," he exhaled and tapped the ashes into the toilet. "But her ol' man never showed up.

"That's crazy! Here I am, mad because my sister didn't bring my daughter like she promised. And you got some guys refusing visits?"

"Oh, you got kids, Youngsta?"

"Yeah, my daughter turned eleven today and I got two boys." I opened my desk drawer and grabbed an envelope full of pictures. I showed Willie my family and introduced him to each of my kids.

When he got to the photo with my mom and sister from last Easter, he paused. He moved the picture closer to his face and then pointed at Brandi. "Yeah, this is the girl I seen in the visiting room."

"You're lying." Shock resonated in my body and caused me to quiver.

"No. I'm fo-sho. That was her."

Anger brewed inside me like a tropical whirlwind and suppressed my curiosity. I sat back and tried to put everything together. When the second-shift C.O., Ms. Curtis, released the unit for chow, I stayed behind. As one of the few officers that respected us as human beings instead of dogging us for our crimes, I asked for her help.

"Excuse me, C.O. I expected a visitor today that didn't come through. Can you check on that for me?"

"Sure."

Later that night, I was microwaving popcorn on the range, when Ms. Curtis put a bug in my ear.

"The first-shift C.O. said that you weren't around."

"Thank you."

The next morning, when Lumscull popped open the doors, I was the first one on the range. I walked up to his desk. He leaned back in the wheeled chair with his fingers locked behind his head.

"Yeah, what you need, Thomas?"

"This!" I punched him in the center of his chin. He fell out of the chair and it slid across the concrete floor. I knelt over him and landed blow after blow. Someone tackled me to the ground. I rolled on top of him, fist ready to strike and then realized that it was Willie.

The prison alarm sounded. Within seconds, officers flooded the unit and ordered everyone to lock it down. When Willie and I got back to the cell, he grabbed me and threw me against the wall. Pressed between his forearm and the cinder blocks, I forced air in and out of my tight lips. My nostrils flared with each breath.

"Why you keep letting them get the best of you, Youngsta? You're already here for killing someone and now you want to beat this guard half to death. You'll never be free until you learn to control your anger!"

At first, his words made no sense. This is the same dude who took on nine C.O.s and knocked out three of them before it was over. But I could see how he was different from what I had pictured. He had a calmness about him — weird for a legendary cop killer / knock-out artist.

He released me from his grip and began to tell me about his case, when the officers rushed into the cell. They cuffed me and then escorted me to solitary confinement, "the hole."

This incident marked my third fight in two years. I knew they would raise my security level and ride me out to Lucasville for the rest of my sentence. Or worse yet, add time for the assault. Instead, the panel gave me nine months in solitary. Word on the block was that Ms. Curtis wrote a statement in my favor explaining the visit.

Later in the week, I received a letter from Willie.

Do not be deceived; evil company corrupts good habits. Awake to righteousness and do not sin; for some do not have the knowledge of God. I speak this to your shame. Behold, I tell you a mystery; we shall not all sleep, but we shall all be changed.

As tough as I am supposed to be, I cried. I wanted that change to happen. Not to make anyone happy, but for me. Every week I looked forward to Willie's letters; quoting Scriptures and inspiring me. I found the same calmness inside myself that shined so bright through him.

Upon release from isolation, oddly enough they allowed me to return to the cell I shared with Willie. Since I only had two months left, he took me under his wing. He showed me "the way" and broke down the rules of this game we play — LIFE.

I looked to Willie as a father figure, something new for me since my father wasn't around. This man was something else. He knew everything. What puzzled me the most was how he knew that I had killed someone. I never asked him about it, but thinking back on it now, I should have.

~ ~ ~ ~ ~ ~ ~

On my day of freedom, I bounced around the cell like a child at Christmas. After chow, I rushed back to the unit to catch Willie before he went to work. I wanted to thank him one last time before I left for home.

When I walked into the cell, he got up from his bunk and walked toward me.

"Youngsta, you ready to be free? It's time to go home."

I wrapped my arms around him. "Willie, I..." A sharp pain sliced through my right rib cage. I released my surrogate father and looked down to see a jagged blade clenched in his hand. Light-headed, my knees buckled and I slid down the cell wall.

Willie pulled a cigarette and a hand-drawn card from his shirt pocket. He stood over me and opened the card. It read "Happy Father's Day, Love Eric." He laid the card on my chest.

With my breathing labored, the puzzle was complete. Eric was the guy I killed eight years ago. All the anger that had imprisoned me vanished. As I laid dying, for the first time in my life, I felt free.

"C.O.! Need to get the medics," Willie said. He then kicked back on his bunk and calmly smoked a cigarette.

The Jewel of Purpose
By Michael Steptoe

Six a.m., following morning cleanliness, I caught the reflection in the mirror. The length of his stare opened a door into the depths of my being. It was there that I, for the first time, witnessed the raw, true image of self. I closed my eyes and held tight to the knot that rose in my throat. When I regained focus, I discovered the reflection had tears that cascaded down his face.

He whispered, "What is the purpose of your life? Where are you headed? Why do you exist? How much do you love me?"

While traveling on this intense quest of self-seeking, I concluded that my search for *things* became the very element that empowered me to seek purpose and commitment. I adopted this principle and grew to understand that my issues were not problems in themselves, but the windows through which I viewed them. How could this be for an individual of many goals?

Although goals are certainly important markers on your journey, you and I are in this world for reasons that transcend the accomplishments of any goal. The purpose for our lives is far grander and more significant than we might have considered. That missing something; that emptiness I experienced was caused by a lack of purpose: the absence of any compelling reason to live.

As I continued to make connections within, it came to me that the overall purpose of my life is to contribute, to serve and to reach beyond self to make a difference in this world. The passion and emotions that accompanied this insight overwhelmed me. I cannot recall being more moved, more hurt, yet more inspired. The experience held a special quality; a wholeness, integrity. An incredible surge of power repositioned somewhere deep within me.

At times, you just know when something is right. This was one of those moments. I understood that my life was important and whatever contribution I make is necessary and needed. In the presence of more than seven billion inhabitants on this planet, my individual existence matters, as does yours.

Security, prosperity, fulfillment, love, peace and harmony are on the goal list for many of us. However, they are not goals, but the results of choice; a commitment to a way of life. While goals nourish the heart, it is purpose that feeds the soul. Hold fast to the thought that your life matters.

Consider those who have earned our modern world's respect: Nelson Mandela, Michail Gorbachev, Harriet Tubman, Malcom X, Oprah, Dr. Martin Luther King, Jr. and J.F.K. Each has different beliefs, callings, careers and direction and we will never agree with all of their objectives. Yet, they have one commonality among them, the power of purpose.

For what purpose were you created? A question only you can answer. No one can hand you a sense of purpose, but keep in mind that it is a sense. More than a rational conclusion, it is instinctive and intuitive. The answer requires a search beyond the mind to the core of one's heart and soul, by way of truth. Our bond lies in the common desire to discover a purpose worthy of our deepest commitment.

Having a purpose for my life has not been a panacea for happiness or a perpetual good feeling. It has however, been a foundational answer to what makes life worthwhile, no matter how dark the challenges.

All my life I've admired my mother's confidence to move forward, take risks, live the life she's envisioned for herself.

My brother and I often refer to her as our Afro-Superwoman. Parents would love to teach their children the power of purpose. Unfortunately, it can't be taught. This treasure must be sought in the core of one's *self*. When this jewel is discovered, its power will enrich your perspective of life, while its growth breaks our minds free from the prison of captive thoughts.

Now as I view myself in the mirror, I stand grateful of what I see. I trust him. I love him. I believe in him. I'm committed to his power of purpose in manifestation as a nurturing father, a responsible son and a productive citizen leading by example.

As I impart to you my life-changing experience, I sit at a cell desk in Ross Correctional Institution. Yet my future has never been brighter. I'm prepared to mentally spread my wings that I may soar through the skies of life. I won't wait for freedom that success may find me. Commitment and purpose now blow as the consistent wind beneath my wings, thus my mental flights embrace success daily.

We were created as a magnificent miracle. At the core of this miracle rests the priceless jewel of life's meaning — the jewel of purpose.

Searching for Change
By James Turner

Change begins within. I had difficultly becoming a better person because full of bitterness, I blamed everyone else for my mistakes. When I was tired of being tired, I faced the truth about myself and the world around me. I acknowledged that I was the one who needed to change to better my circumstances. I realized that once I changed, everything around me would change.

I have not always weighed the cost and benefits of my actions, but since being incarcerated, I am learning how to be responsible and accountable for my actions. I now understand that the choices and decisions that I make do not just affect me because what affects one directly, affects us all indirectly. Therefore, it is vital that I do not just make good choices and decisions, but the best choices and decisions. I will not be thinking just for myself, but for those around me.

March 2000, I was twenty-five years old and facing 160 years to life, a direct result of negative thinking, destructive behavior and my misconception that the world revolved around me. I did not fully understand what life meant until faced with spending the rest of my life in prison. After sitting in the County Jail for seven months, fighting not to spend the rest of my life in prison, I received a ten-year sentence. Ten years is a long time, but it was a much smaller number than the three-digit score of a basketball game gone into double overtime that was originally presented to me.

For me to compare the things that I was about to lose, to all of the things that I had taken, would have been unfair. To put a value on priceless things and say, "I am sorry," would not have been enough. My mental, spiritual and emotional struggle — caused by my own selfishness — was too much burden even for my worst enemy. Not to mention the affect of my actions on loved ones and society.

I reached a crossroad: live or die. I chose to live. To do so, I changed my attitude, thinking and behavior not conducive to the change that I needed and wanted to make in my life.

One of the first things that I did was draw closer to God. A poor decision placed me face-to-face with the realization that I needed strength from a higher power. I had witnessed time and time again that something greater than I had to achieve the change and renewal of my mind. I decided that regardless of what happened I would start making better choices and decisions and weigh the costs and benefits of my actions. It was not hard to see that my decisions cost me more than they benefited me. The numbers just weren't adding up.

I had taken so much from family, friends, society and myself that the only way to right even a small portion of my wrongs was to help others avoid the same mistakes. A wise man learns from the experiences of others rather than suffer through the pain caused from his bad choices. I decided to share my experiences and apply effective solutions that could be used to deter others headed in the same direction.

I will have to play many different roles on this journey through life. However, how I will respond to and handle these roles is up to me. The lessons taught in the midst of my most trying times have made me aware that I will have to be prepared for the obstacles that I will encounter. If I become comfortable in one state of mind or pattern of thinking my growth will be stagnated and limited. Placing myself inside a box to prohibit change could be detrimental. Life is forever changing.

I am not the same person I was a year ago, or even yesterday. I have grown. I no longer allow my perception of reality to be clouded or tainted by the strongholds of instant gratification, justification of right and wrong or any thinking that led me to believe that I did not need to change. As a different person, my cognitive skills, attitude and behavior have changed and complement the new me.

Prison life is what one makes of it. You can either use it as a time to grow and get in touch with God and self or you can rot and leave worse than when you came. I chose to use this as a time to grow and face truths about myself. I am far from perfect. Sometimes I do not represent who I desire to become, but I will not lose. I will not give up. Nothing beats a failure but a try.

Prison is a school and can serve as a means of higher learning. It taught me about consequences when I make poor choices and decisions. Prison has also taught me how to make better choices, address my emotions and attitudes and deal with people from all walks of life. This instructor has permitted me to see and appreciate the things I once took for granted; taking a bath or hearing the newspaper hit the porch in the morning. It does not matter if my intentions are good. I still have to confront self and apply positive actions if I expect to get positive results.

Without exercising caution and setting pride and ego aside, prison can create a monster. My pride and ego can taint and cloud my vision to the point where I believe that I am not the problem. I focus on the positive lessons that this experience teaches me, however, I never lose sight of the negatives. Why? Because I cannot change if I do not remember the person I once was. A thin line exists between the two, so I use my negatives to ignite my positives — the combination is my catalyst for change.

I am a work in progress because room for improvement is ever present. The Greek philosopher, Socrates, said, "The unexamined life of man is not worth living." I relate to that philosophy because as I allowed negative thinking to manifest negative actions, I failed to examine the consequences of my recklessness.

During my incarceration, I have taken several programs and a course of action that produced a constructive change in my life. Hope for change was not enough. I had to want a change, think positive and then allow my actions to follow. I had to cultivate and bear the fruit of the seeds of change that were planted in me.

Most importantly, I continue to take life-changing steps by learning to look for the good in even the worst situations; one attribute of a mature, critical thinker. I think outside the box and look at the bigger picture. I am beginning to understand that no matter the circumstances, I can persevere and overcome all the things that once held me back. I can now deal with my negative thinking and fear of change.

This process has not just been heart wrenching for me, but has also caused my family indescribable pain. It created a void in time that can never be filled. I think beyond getting out of prison; I think about getting out and staying out. I have set short-term goals that will prepare and enable me to reach the long-term goal: stay out of prison by becoming a productive member of society. I choose to be the best son, brother and father that I can be. I choose to stand and be the creator of my successful and happy ending.

The Seed of Karma

By Charles "Chill Will" Williams
Dedicated to Ashley Wongus. I love and miss you eternally.

I never intended to become a convicted felon, much less a murderer. However, three months after turning twenty-one, my freedom was at stake as a prosecutor suggested I serve a fifteen-to-life sentence. *Fifteen to life?* I recited mentally, repeating the words of a court-appointed lawyer as he explained what was told to him. My calm expression transcended into one of defiance as my brows lowered. The fury within me made my heart beat a bit harder than normal.

"I was defending myself," I said, as I slammed my fists on the table. "The investigators even acknowledged that I wasn't the aggressor. How could I face so much time?"

"Mr. Williams, it's likely that there will be a reduction of the charges, accompanied by a plea bargain for a much lighter sentence." He gathered his documents sprawled across the table and stuffed them into his briefcase. "Although you weren't the aggressor, you violated your duty to retreat. And the number of times you fired---"

"The man attacked me with a machete! What else was I supposed to do?"

Despite the given responsibility for causing a man's death, the only victim my mind envisioned was me. No part of the matter at hand was my fault. From my perspective — originally, at least — I had been wronged the most. Amidst the battle to displace the guilt that was solely my own, finding myself to blame was unfathomable. It never occurred to me that I deserved to suffer the backlash of this situation. Karma had finally caught up with me.

As is true of most, I have struggled spiritually with sins committed so often that they soon became routine. Yet the largest hurdle set along my path has always been fornication. I was an addict. Promiscuity had me bound with the strength and endurance of steel shackles and chains, making it seemingly impossible to break free. The desire for freedom never existed. I enjoyed the indulgences of my life and found the thrill of unprotected sex as fulfilling as the risks. It was sickening, by far. Nevertheless, it was my life.

Fornication evolved into an addiction similar to one induced by drugs. The only difference; I seldom settled for the first fix. I obtained a high by setting my primary focus on women who were involved in relationships — preferably serious ones. A single woman was not a challenge, but a woman deeply in love with her mate was indeed a conquest in the making. Regardless of how content a woman claimed to be, my objective was to identify an area in her relationship where her man fell short. I then led her astray from any thoughts of happiness with her current courtship. The excitement of the hunt, the pursuit of the chase, the desire to have what was deemed forbidden, just for the sake of having it. Such desires ignited the force that drove me to snatch away the girlfriends of many; from total strangers to relatives and associates. With a few phone conversations, I found myself spending more intimate time with a woman than the man to whom she was devoted.

Various encounters witnessed by other children introduced me to sex at a young age. As for the hunger to seduce an involved woman, its starting point escapes me. Yet, there remains one distinct recollection. My mother unveiled the unforgettable revelation that the man I knew as Charles Williams, Jr. was not my biological father. Rather, he was the individual to whom my mother was married and I was the product of an extramarital affair. Fourteen years old and unable to cope with the hurt from years of deceit created my justification: I'm just like my daddy then. It's in my genes to ruin relationships. Believing that lie fueled me to continue the pattern — one that came with quite a price.

Raised, saved, and baptized within the holy dwellings of the Pentecostal church, one would classify my lifestyle as shameful. From an inward prospective, no one knew better than I that my doings were ungodly. Even so, the cycle evolved further upon making the acquaintance of Michelle, a married woman. Choosing to be involved with her was not only a sacrilegious move that produced an adulterer, but was also the starting point for the undoing of my life at its seams.

Our innocent beginnings stemmed from my friendship with Michelle's niece. Through that relationship, Michelle and her spouse came to know me from phone calls and occasional visits. Michelle and I exchanged no flirtatious comments or flattering looks, however everything changed the morning I received a phone call from her.

"Hi, Michelle. What's up? Did your niece give you my number?"

"No, I memorized it from the caller ID." She sighed and then continued. "I need some company."

I checked my watch and noted that it wasn't yet 8:00 a.m. "Company? Where's your husband?"

"At work."

I contemplated whether to decline or accept the invitation. Brief consideration allowed me to accept and our morning calls occurred two to five times a week.

Michelle and I disregarded the Lord's seventh commandment for over a year without regret. Beyond the intimacy and emotional support, portions of her husband's

95

earnings fell into my hands as well. On occasion, I chose her groceries — some of which she prepared and served to me. The affair gained so much depth that I talked Michelle out of leaving her husband for me several times.

Blinded by my sin, the downward slope my life traveled included a gloomy mood, loosened ties with family and frequent smoking. An untamed temper resulted in my termination from a lucrative job as a certified station cook.

My career's demise led me to work as an unlicensed cab driver. I drove my 1989 Thunderbird to the spot for independent cabbies — Over the Rhine — and waited on fares. Since I chose to work the night shift, I carried a handgun for protection. Bits and pieces of a once prosperous life fell apart, destined to dwindle further and pave the way to disaster.

~ ~ ~ ~ ~ ~ ~

Three in the morning, a woman hailed me for a ride. She jumped in the front seat and slammed the door.

"I need to get to Westwood as fast as possible."

"Yes, ma'am." I adjusted the rearview mirror and drove off.

Five minutes into the ride, she got a call on her cell phone. "Baby, I'm on my way. I'll be there in about fifteen minutes." The man on the other line yelled so loud that she pulled the phone away from her ear. She listened without interrupting the barrage of profanities until he hung up. "Oh, Lord." She fell back into the seat and mumbled something under her breath.

Fifteen minutes later we arrived at her requested destination. A man stepped off the sidewalk on the other side of the street and walked toward the car. My passenger exited the cab, tossed a ten-dollar bill through the open driver-side window and then stood by the car.

"You a cab driver," the sidewalk man inquired.

I nodded. Given the abrasive phone conversation and current I'm-tired-of-this-mess stance, I discreetly reached for the gun stashed under the seat. I palmed the weapon in my hand just as he drew a three-foot blade from behind his back.

"Get out the car!" He moved closer. "You've been sleeping with my wife, while I'm home watching our kids." He lifted the machete above his head and stepped closer to the car. "You won't wreck another home!" He swung the blade into the vehicle.

True enough, his accusations were characteristic of me, however I hadn't displayed them toward the love of his life.

The five shots didn't grant me a prison term for voluntary manslaughter, nor did the seven-month run from the law — hell on earth. This entire matter was due to my past dealings. The seed of karma had been sown in fertile soil and its harvest was inevitable. Although the woman was a total stranger whom I hadn't touched or flirted with, many in my past had fallen unfaithful at my hands. I got what was coming. That's how karma works. I didn't decipher this revelation until I was well into my incarceration.

Four years into my prison term, Michelle — still married — remained the only woman to stay in touch. Her lustful letters, revealing photos, money orders and visits soothed my pain of imprisonment, but a larger matter remained unaddressed. My soul was sick. I prayed for God's forgiveness and severed all ties with Michelle. I vowed to myself to never touch an involved woman again. The loneliness that ensued consumed me, but was much deserved. It did not compare to the pain that I created in a union formed by God. Such pain simulated the wound of a double-edged sword; injuring not only Michelle and her marriage, but me and my life. Frankly, I am still healing.

Valerie L. Coleman

For Better, For Worse, For Prison
By Kimberly Scott
Written by Valerie L. Coleman

When I took my marriage vows in 1986, I never anticipated the "for better or for worse" promise would land me in prison.

My marriage started out like a fairytale: a loving husband, two beautiful children, a comfortable life. And then my husband started using crack. No longer my knight in shining armor, he became violent and abusive. I loved him with all that I had in me, but it was not enough. Over the course of several years, his mood swings caused him to lose his job and in 1993, he left me to raise our son and daughter alone.

During our separation, he met a woman and in two months, she was pregnant. Still in love with my husband, I accepted his request to come home and "work things out." Although we shared the same home, we didn't have much of a relationship. I tried to be a loving wife, but resentment had settled in my heart.

On Mother's Day 1994, I gave my life to the Lord. He met me at my lowest and ministered to my hurt. Two months later, my husband's second son was born. When his son was thirteen months old, my husband brought him to the apartment. The toddler cried and lifted his hands out for me. I picked him up, looked into his brown eyes and from that moment I raised him as my own. The mothering transition was not easy. I had no desire to rear another child as a single parent — my husband and I were more like roommates. And although I was saved and loved the Lord, He forced me to pray for His guidance. He wanted to order my steps.

The baby's biological mother called on occasion and came by to visit her son, but she never took him to live with her.

Most people believed that he was my birth child and I didn't tell them any different.

Over time, my husband's behavior became erratic. He started an internet business and the "sales rep" came to our house to set-up his Website. Looking back at it now, I believe that's when he started selling drugs. The transactions did not occur in our home because he was seldom there, but in my heart I now suspect this business was a front.

The verbal and physical abuse escalated on the few nights my husband came home. When he didn't come around for weeks at a time, the struggles of life abused me. Maintaining a home, parenting three small children alone, trying to hold down a job and keeping my sanity overwhelmed me. Between the midnight tears and daylight fears, I sought the Lord.

One morning, as I prepared for work, the Lord spoke to me.

Kim, I loved you when you didn't love Me. Now you love him, like I loved you. Come back to your first love. Come back to Me.

In the summer of 2000, my husband informed me that he found a home and we were moving. He also told me that I would have to pay the rent, phone and utilities. Given the history of abuse whenever I challenged his authority, I agreed. One benefit to the move was that it put me less than fifteen minutes from my church, Solid Rock Church (SRC). I needed as much time in the presence of the King and His children as I could get.

I often asked my husband how we could afford the lavish home. With malice in his eyes, he replied, "None of your business." I eventually accepted our lifestyle and paid the bills as instructed. Treated more like an evil stepsister than his wife, our relationship continued to deteriorate.

December 2004, I took my children out for some after-Christmas shopping. When we arrived home, two police officers greeted me in the driveway.

They followed me inside and questioned me about my husband's illicit activities. Since they were men of the law, I felt safe and cooperated without having an attorney present. Hindsight now tells me that they did not care about me in the least. Their objective was to bring down my husband by any means necessary.

"Ma'am, as long as your husband cooperates with us, you have nothing to worry about."

I'm sure that it was the pending trial, but my husband began to treat me better. He apologized for how he had mistreated me over the years and joined me at church on several occasions. Things were looking up, but everything looks up when you're at the bottom.

I was indicted in April 2005 and spent six days in the Warren County Jail. I was released on a $5,000 bond and then my father-in-law retained an attorney for me.

My lawyer took a pen out his inside jacket pocket. "Mrs. Scott, I know that you didn't have anything to do with your husband's crimes. I also know that as a victim of abuse, you submitted to his demands." He scribbled some notes on his legal pad and then continued. "We will take you to trial after your husband. I expect that the courts will be lenient with you given the situation."

My husband's two-day trial was held in late October 2005. On the second day, the court told my husband that he was facing fifty-five years if found guilty. The jury went to deliberate around lunch time, so the trial was scheduled to reconvene three hours later. The judge, court reporter, jury and attorneys all returned for deliberation. My husband did not. Almost three hours passed before they realized he had fled.

Recalling the words of the officer, I feared that my husband's lack of cooperation would be held against me.

My attorney encouraged. "Not to worry. We are going to use his history of domestic violence on your behalf. You'll be fine."

On November 22, 2005, I was found guilty of cocaine trafficking, a felony. When I left the courthouse that evening, my husband's picture was posted on the prosecuting attorney's office door. The next morning, when I returned for sentencing, his picture was gone. I received a mandatory three-year sentence, a $10,000 fine and revocation of my driver's license.

I thank God for my church family. They had supported me throughout the trial and sentencing. With only thirty days to file an appeal, one of the members sought the services of a fellow saint and attorney — a Godsend.

I left for Marysville, an Ohio prison for women, on December 2. I spent the first thirty-five days in a holding bin called Hale Cottage — *Hell* Cottage is more exact. Now housing three hundred women together is bad enough, but telling those women when to eat, sleep and pee is a whole other matter.

One of my first bunkmates was a young girl who was two months pregnant. When she arrived, the institution doctor could not find a heartbeat for her baby. They scheduled her for a dilation and curettage (D & C) without getting a second opinion.

"Something in my heart tells me that you are still pregnant," I said to her before lights out.

"Why do you say that? The doctors think my baby is dead."

101

"I'm not sure, but things aren't adding up. You haven't been sick and you don't have the odor of death."

For the next two weeks, she had to climb to the top bunk. We prayed often. The day she was scheduled to go to the hospital at Ohio State University, the nurse wanted to check her one last time. You already know. They heard the baby's heartbeat and sent the young lady back to her bunk. Praise the Lord! She asked me for a Bible and I helped her get one. During my stay at Marysville, I watched that young lady give her life to the Lord within the walls of prison.

From Hell Cottage, we were separated by crime and security level. My offense placed me at the lowest threat level and into Kennedy I Cottage as one of 175 women. Everyone had a work assignment or went to school to earn $20 a month. Lying around in bed all day was not an option. My job was in Big Laundry. I visited each cottage and collected large laundry bags, with up to 300 pounds of dirty clothes, and carted them to the laundry room for servicing. The high security women, identified with pink shirts and locked in at all times, washed, dried and folded the clothes. Once laundered, I returned the items to the respective cottages.

As the new kid on the block, a seasoned inmate set me up for trouble. When I made the rounds to pick up laundry bags, this female tucked her blanket in with the clothes. Institution policy did not allow for the laundering of blankets because they were too heavy for the machines. Unaware that the blanket was in the cart, I rolled it over to the laundry. The blanket was washed and then staged in the storage unit since no one knew who owned it. The next day, the female saw me in the yard.

"Do you have my stuff?"

"What stuff?"

"You know what stuff."

"I have no idea what you're talking about. You should go to Big Laundry and ask the officer about your stuff." I left for work. I asked around, located her blanket and returned to her cottage. Not thinking like a criminal, I handed her the blanket in front of a corrections officer.

"What are you doing," the officer asked.

"I'm returning her blanket."

"And just how did you get her blanket?"

"It was in Big Laundry."

"And how did it get to Big Laundry?"

This series of questions continued for some time. The officer did not believe that I was innocent. Can't say that I blame him given my current residency. Our conversation got louder and then he called me a punk. By this time, other inmates came to my defense and tried to convince him that I didn't intentionally do anything wrong.

Frustrated with the outpouring of support, the officer looked at me and said, "Shut up and sit down. I'll deal with you later." He had every intention of having me put in the hole, standard protocol for this offense.

My bunkmate confronted the female and told her that if I go to the hole, then my bunkmate would also have to go. And if that happened, things would not be good for the female. The woman that slept in the bunk next to me said that she would sit with me day and night like Job's friends to encourage me.

When officers for the next shift arrived, they questioned me and then released me back to my bunk. They knew the female had a history of trying to get over on the system and believed my story. She slept without sheets for the weekend. Doesn't sound like much of a punishment, but trust me, it is.

A routine part of institutionalization is periodic physicals. On one occasion, the results of my blood sugar came back at

300 — way too high to be healthy. The medical staff insisted that I take some medicine to reduce my blood sugar to a more acceptable level.

"I'm not taking that medicine."

"And why not? We're only trying to help you." The doctor seemed agitated by my refusal.

"I don't know a lot about medicine, but I do know that that stuff causes diarrhea."

"Well, yes it does, however you have access to the restroom."

"Not really. The C.O.s don't let us use the restroom freely. I'll mess myself waiting on them to let me go." I hadn't been locked up for long, but I had observed them denying restroom privileges on numerous occasions. Not for any particular reason, except that they could. The officers shut down toilets by placing tape over them. At one point, eight stalls were rendered unusable. Can you imagine 175 women limited to using two toilets? Not a pretty picture.

The doctor was at a loss for words, so the nurse commented. "Do you want to kill yourself?"

"Like I said before, I know enough about medicine to know that I will wait until I'm in the general population to take it." My insolence could have landed me in the hole, but God. Instead, the doctor had me complete an Against Medical Advice form. I wrote why I refused the medicine. In three days, the tape was removed from the toilets. To my knowledge, that control tactic has not been used again.

While I was "on lock down," I did not have any visitors. As a result, no one could send me boxes of food or clothes. My church family rallied together and sent money that was applied to my account. I used the money to purchase personal items for myself and my bunkmate. She did not receive any outside money and the monthly work earnings didn't last through the month. I ran the risk of going to the hole by blessing her, but I considered it my tithes.

I attended church regularly and my bunkmate often joined me. I witnessed her give her life to the Lord. We had a friend who was Catholic. Although she didn't attend church with me, she promised to attend when my home church, SRC, came to the prison for ministry. As she promised, she joined us for service and said that she felt the presence of the Lord. Upon her release, she plans to visit us.

The written code in prison is that officers are not allowed to touch inmates even if they are in physical distress. For example, if an inmate has violent convulsions during a seizure, an officer cannot do anything to keep her from hurting herself. He had to wait for backup. In the two to five minutes it took for help to arrive, the woman could have seriously injured herself. So the other inmates restrained and protected her from bashing her head on the concrete floor — the unwritten code. Although the officers weren't permitted to help, they didn't want us to help either. Some women have been punished for trying to help a sister.

During my stay in Kennedy I, I met Barb. Her infirmities rendered her helpless at times, so I cared for her when she couldn't care for herself.

"Why are you here," she asked one day, when I kept her from rolling off the bed. "Your spirit does not belong here. You're trustworthy."

~ ~ ~ ~ ~ ~ ~

I asked my attorney to file an appeal bond. He indicated that the courts do not normally do this, but he would oblige me. The appeal sat on the judge's desk for almost two months, but in April 2006, the appeal was approved. All I needed was $6,000 cash and $60,000 in property. Now where was I going to get that kind of collateral? My father gave the money and a family at my church, whom I'd only met as a worker in the children's ministry, put up a house for me.

On May 8, 2006, I was brought before the County magistrate to hear the conditions of the bond. After a series of "It's not my job" blunders with paperwork, I was released the next day.

Within a week, I had a part-time job at Dr. Patrick Spencer's office. While incarcerated, a nurse friend vouched for my work ethic. She told the doctor that she would bet her job on me. I have been employed with this office for over a year and am now full-time status. When I left the prison, I needed glasses. Guess what type of medicine Dr. Spencer practices — ophthalmology —the treatment of eyes. I have 20/20 vision now thanks to my new glasses. Praise Him!

I've had several hearings since my release and in March 2007 I won my appeal. I have not heard from my husband, but I pray for him daily. I believe that God is working on him wherever he may be. As for me, I am anxiously awaiting the day when the Lord manifests Himself in the dismissal of my case.

I know that God will replace everything we lose to the enemy. And when He puts His plan in motion, even the devil in hell can't stop it. I encourage you to trust Him in all things.

Lean not unto your own understanding, but in all your ways acknowledge Him and He will direct your path.

~ Proverbs 3:5-6

If You Find an Open Door, Walk Through It

By Adele Nieves

An interview with an anonymous woman who has been in and out of the prison system since she was fourteen years old.

Tell me a little about yourself.

I'm thirty-two years old and grew up in an urban area on the East Coast. My grandmother raised me because my mother was a heroin addict and she was always going in and out of jail. My father was off doing his own thing and never worried about me or his other children.

It was hard growing up with my grandmother. If it had started out that way, and that was all I knew, it would have been fine. But my mother took me back a number of times. I saw another life with my mother and it seemed like an easier life: easy money, no responsibility, no one to answer to, hanging out all night at the town pool or in the streets. It was simpler and fun.

My dad would reappear every once in a while. He staggered into the house drunk or high, have a violent temper tantrum, beat me up and then go on his way. When my mother got caught stealing or hustling, she went back to jail. I was shipped back to my grandmother — back to a curfew, homework, chores and responsibilities.

The back and forth was emotionally hard. I felt like no one wanted me, like I was always being kicked to the curb. That's where my destructive behavior started. I sabotaged anything good that came into my life because I felt like I didn't deserve it.

This was my first experience of life, of what a family looked like. I was birthed into suffering. No one ever explained the difference between right and wrong. Maybe I saw it in others, but no one ever sat me down and talked to me; reinforced it.

<u>What was so attractive about the streets? What was out there that provided comfort?</u>

Money! Money brings the friends, the clothes, the drugs, the booze, and [the illusion of] love. I didn't see another way to get what I could get with money. It was the root to everything; to my comfort and my love.

I hustled to keep friendships. I put myself on the line. I put myself in danger to buy people's love just to have them like me. Whatever I had, I gave it away. Or I'd take something to give it away; it didn't matter what it was. I've never gone to jail for me. I've been in jail four summers in a row. I have not had one free summer in years and it was because others were greedy off my back. I was never selfish for me. I stole food and clothes for other women's children then the minute their situation changed, they forgot about me.

It takes time to grow up. I've finally grown up and seen the light.

<u>Why couldn't you get out?</u>

It was all I knew. I was weak, disguised as street smart. Some people wake up in the morning and go to work. I woke up to work on the streets. That was my only way of living. Once you're in it you can't get out, unless you have someone on your side. You need support. I got lucky. I had support. It's the one thing I needed.

On the streets when you have money, you have "friends" that say they would die for you. In normal life you don't have friends like that. That becomes your "school."

When the chips were down and I didn't have money, [crime] was the only way I knew how to get it. I have an extensive background in getting money the easy way, the fast way. I learned it by watching my mom, a lesson that she passed down to me.

When I'm on the streets, I have fun like I'm in a college dorm. You hang out and you don't think about tomorrow. It's the same as jail. I'm not devastated like most people would be in jail. I'm hanging with the same people I hung with on the streets. The difference is that in jail I have a guaranteed three meals a day.

You've been in jail more than once. Why do you think that is?

I first went to jail at fourteen and I've been in and out since eighteen. I remember going to court one Easter Sunday. That's how I celebrated Easter. Why? Because I'm a career criminal. Sometimes I get greedy and other times I get pushed into it. I wasn't ready to end the lifestyle and you have to be ready.

What is it like in County Jail?

In County, you have less of a life. You are on four lockdowns a day because so many people are coming in and out. You have head counts three times a day. It's one big room with like 150 girls. You don't have the freedom to hang in the yard. You are definitely behind bars. It's different than prison. You go to prison if you have to do over a year of time. In prison, you get to go out in the yard and you have opportunities to work toward something. Most people would prefer prison, but I'm not recommending either!

What do you think the other women in the system fear the most?

A lot of them fear never seeing their kids again. It's my same fear. Most of the women I met were also career criminals. The only thing that is real is your kids, your family. That's where your emotions come in.

What do you wish you did differently?

I wish I would have stayed in school. I could have tried for a career, a decent job.

I wish I didn't sabotage everything good. I couldn't accept that they wouldn't abandon me too. When you work for what you buy, when you earn what you buy, you treasure things. There's real value in them. For me, things and people are dispensable. I have dispensed of them all.

I wish my parents would have just left me alone. I followed my mother's path and I wish I never saw that life. I didn't want to be like her, but the lessons were already ingrained. Everyday is a hustle. You never relax. You're always looking over your shoulder, so you never learn to appreciate the time you have.

How and when did you decide to take a different path; to get your life on track?

I got caught up in this because I wanted to give. The only way I knew how to give something was by taking from someone and giving it to someone else. But I've learned a new way of doing that. I'm so lucky. Others out there don't have what I have, but you have to look around and take notice of what is real. Everyone has something. It can be family, a good friend, a center, or even your children.

What I did differently... the last time I went to jail I looked around and saw old ladies in jail. I realized that I didn't want to be an old lady still in and out of jail, or permanently there. I decided to take an anger management class. In that class, someone talked to me for the first time. I got knowledge about the things and issues going on inside of me. They gave me tools. I got to see that I was special, I had good things. But I was also ready for this change. And then I wanted to hold my daughter and just be with her. Just be.

When you take a class like that, so much awareness comes to you. It took one class to open me up, be willing to talk. I woke up everyday and made sure I got to class. If you want it bad enough, you'll find a way to get out.

When I got out of jail, I took that knowledge from class and went to a community organization that does outreach education. They offered a year-long survey program for people with AIDS or minorities who just got out of jail. I don't have AIDS, but I am a minority. I made it happen.

They gave me everything I needed: clothes, food, shelter, tools to find a job, tools to integrate into life and stay out of jail. If you need a bus pass to get somewhere, they give it to you, but you have to do the footwork. You got to put your work into it. They give you the ways; they give you the counseling, the therapy. Anything you can possibly need to go out there and live.

I did everything I had to do. I won't lie. I slipped about four months in. I was lonely. I didn't have friends in this new, awkward life and I searched for the hustle again. And then I got a visit from a counselor. Since I don't lie, I told him that I slipped. He gave me numbers to call, and where and how to go for therapy. Again, I have to do the work and I'm doing it because I know where I'm going if I don't. I can't do that again, I can't do that time. I can't lose my life, my mind! As tough as I seem, I'm scared.

I got my GED in jail and now I'm taking classes to be a veterinary assistant. I never thought I'd have a real job or a normal life. But I can see it now for the first time in my life. I want to be happy. I never knew what that meant.

Do you have any advice for girls/women who may be heading in the same direction you took?

I can't give the kind of advice you're looking for. I had people giving me good, solid advice, but I didn't listen. What I can say is get out while you can. If you find an open door, walk through it.

Dig deep and want the help. There's no way of getting the help unless you want it. Part of doing time, being on the streets, losing your time, is wanting someone to notice you. That want is there, you need to seek the support in a different way. Take that talent you have for the hustle and hustle for you. Focus on something you find beautiful; that inspires you. It doesn't matter what it is. For me, it's nature, the beach and animals. So now I spend a lot of time seeking those things out. Get lost in that kind of beauty; find your beauty.

Do you have any final words?

Yes. I believe there is a God. As long as you have faith in the Lord, everything is possible. I have to admit, without the person above I wouldn't be here right now. When you feel like you have no one, you do have someone. You have Him, Her, It. If you have faith, in whatever form that comes, it'll carry you.

His Promise

By Haylee Ann Montgomery

I sat in shock waiting for my husband, Tim, to be released on bail. The criminal charges against him held a twelve-year maximum sentence. Never in my wildest dreams had I imagined myself here at this place in life. Twenty-four hours earlier, life was normal.

That morning Tim, our three children and I had a birthday breakfast for my nine-year-old son at a local bagel shop. We savored the exotic spreads as we honored him. Minutes after arriving home the police came and took my husband away in handcuffs. Where was God? Surely He saw. Surely He knew. Surely He would act. My heart pounded with a wordless prayer.

That night after Tim was released on bail he held my hand. Tears formed in his eyes as he said, "Thanks for not giving up on me. I don't know what I would do if you abandoned me."

"No. You are stuck with me!" I chuckled.

He squeezed my hand. "Today while I was in the waiting area I had an opportunity to talk with an inmate about God's love. She was amazed. Someone else had recently told her the exact same thing. I told her God was trying to tell her something. She agreed." He hesitated and then whispered, "I think God might be leading me into prison ministry."

Dumbfounded, I cried to God as I said, "Can't You start this ministry from the outside?"

We prayed. Many prayed with us and God listened. He didn't change our circumstance, He changed our hearts. He is Lord and has rights to everything we have. It is His to give and His to take away. And for us — take away it was.

In spite of the sudden turn in our lives, Tim's focus continued to be on others. He always thinks of others — whether it's giving a compassionate listening ear, cutting trees littering a friend's yard, helping our children with frustrating homework or carefully timing his corny jokes to ease another's tension. Quiet self-sacrificing is his way of life. He even built our house with a large, cheery, welcoming living area to inspire good, meaningful conversations. Tim's desires were to house church gatherings and provide a safe, peaceful haven where others could come and be refreshed when beaten and battered by the world. One such family, who had been to our house years before, now stood as Tim's accuser. Even after the accusations, love and concern for them was evident in his speech and prayers. He had a humble acceptance of God's sovereignty even in this situation.

But I trembled. One question resonated through me: If He allowed the worst, how could we stand? What was the secret? I have seen many go through tough periods. Some came through withered, wounded and beaten — never to walk upright again. But others grew strong and came out as gold. What was the difference? I needed to know. I was desperate to know.

I searched the Scriptures, read the Psalms, prayed and sought His face. Then God showed me. He knows I am a visual person, so He gave me a picture. It began with a still shot of Tim in mid-stride. He was walking into a room but his right heel was still outside the room. Then it was as if someone pressed "play" on a remote. Tim's step continued and he disappeared into the room. I knew the room that Tim walked into was the secret shelter of the Most High — the place of protection. Only as he disappeared was Tim shielded and protected. The enemy of our souls could not find him because he was hid with Christ in God.

He that dwells in the shelter of the Most High will abide in the shadow of the Almighty. I will say to the Lord, my refuge and my fortress; my God, in Him I trust!

~ Psalm 91:1-2

The way to enter this room; the secret to entering His protection is to give everything to the Lordship of Christ. Claim Him as "my God" and subject everything to Him. Allow no secret area to harbor sin. God wants to be Lord of everything we own, everything we are and everything we hope to be. At that place, He is fully our refuge, strength and protector.

Trust in the Lord with all your heart. Lean not on your own understanding. Acknowledge Him in all your ways and He will direct your paths.

~ Proverbs 3:5-6

We trusted. We leaned. We acknowledged — at least we were getting better at it. He directed us. He had to because He promised and that left no room for anything else. He whispered into our hearts to keep our eyes on Him. Trust Him. Follow Him. Walk where He tells us to walk. He promised to take care of the rest. No matter where the road led. And the road continued to lead where we did not want to go.

A month later, Tim was ripped away from us again. Whatever happened to innocent before proven guilty? Tim was not allowed to live with or visit us. He could not see us except at church functions. Forcibly separated, Tim had to find another place to live. For some reason, God saw fit to strip us down to full dependence upon Him.

Devastation filled our quiet home the night Tim had to leave. We clung to him with everything in us — trying to make up for the times we wouldn't be able to hug him. He tried to

115

encourage us, but our hearts tore, our eyes continually wet. It felt like we were falling into a deep crevasse. But we had a foundation, this pit had a bottom.

As I put our children, ages seven, nine and ten, to bed that night, my oldest and youngest were inconsolable. I comforted Annie, the youngest, at her bedside until her sobs subsided. I crossed the hall into the boys' room to console Matthew. As I stepped away, Annie's grief overcame her and she sobbed uncontrollably. I comforted Matthew as Annie wailed in the other room. Then I comforted Annie as Matthew sobbed. Then Matthew... I made no headway. The sobbing was heart wrenching. Reduced to tears, I couldn't see anymore.

This is not working. "Group hug!" Matthew and Annie ran to me. We clung to each other.

"Daniel, you too," I said to my resilient middle child.

"Oh Mom, I'm in bed. Do I have to?"

"Yes. We need you."

Daniel reluctantly joined us. Three of us cried and dripped puddles on the rug, clutching each other for comfort.

"Uh, Mom," Daniel whispered. "Have you noticed I'm not crying?"

"Yes, Daniel I did notice that," I said as I wiped away my tears.

"Well, Mom," he said in a matter-of-fact tone. "It's just that I know God is in control and Daddy's okay. He's not alone. God is with him and God is with us. He doesn't leave us. This isn't too big for Him." The faith of a child. How true his words were.

I breathed in the truth. "Daniel, you are absolutely correct. God will be with Daddy and God will be with us. He will always be with us and never leave us. We *can* trust Him. But it is okay to be sad because we miss Daddy. It is okay as long as we know underneath it all God is with us. It's not as deep of a sadness, but it is okay to cry." I had Daniel repeat his statement to make sure that his siblings heard him through their tears. We all realized what Daniel said was true. We do have a hope that is deeper than anything in the world; in every situation and for all time. When the sniffling slowed, I suggested we all sleep in my room. Their faces brightened and we raced to get blankets and pillows.

We learned to live one day at a time. God provided abundant grace for each day, but not in advance. Looking ahead, sometimes we were terrified. God had not yet given us grace for those future days. We soon realized that when the terrifying days come, the grace given is sufficient even then. Streams of grace are there and waiting.

I can do everything through Him who gives me strength.

~ Philippians 4:13

As our ordeal progressed I was asked to see a counselor to satisfy governmental conditions. Our Christianity is not always a plus in their eyes. I had to decide whether to tone it down and hide it or let them know the truth. Now that I look back, there was no choice to make. I could not have hid it if I wanted to. Acknowledging Him is the only way for me.

My counselor used many metaphors. He drew pictures on the board, trying to simplify and explain complex situations. At the end of one session, he asked, "How is it you are doing so well with all that is going on?" His face and question revealed that he was puzzled. In his experience, people just did not walk upright through these types of situations.

"I have a metaphor to describe why I am doing well."

His eyes lit up and he smiled. "Great! Tell me."

"Okay, it's as if there's a cup inside each of us. This cup represents our emotional health and is filled with the knowledge that we are special, we are loved, that we have purpose and hope. When we're doing really well, our cup overflows. We know we are loved, we positively impact our world, we encourage others. When the level in our cup lowers, we may have sad, quiet moments or become anxious. When it gets really low we are basket cases." I stood and picked up the chalk to write on the board. "Unfortunately this cup inside us has a hole at the bottom that continually drips. We are leaky. Every one of us leaks. When times are difficult, pressure pushes down on the cup and we leak faster. During these times we need more poured into us because more leaks out."

I drew a cup with droplets seeping from the bottom. Above the cup, I sketched a pitcher that poured into it. "This leakiness is why I am being so careful to pour into my kids. I try to make sure my kids know that they are loved and special."

"I really like this metaphor," he said. "This is good! Okay, so you are pouring into your kids, but what about you? Who is filling your cup?"

"Ahh, but it's not my responsibility to make sure my kids' cups are overflowing. Sure it's my job and privilege to pour into them, but it is not my responsibility to make sure they are full. That is God's responsibility." I put the chalk down, turned to him and gave him my full attention. "Who is filling my cup? My husband has been ripped away from me, so he cannot pour into my cup like before. But it is not my husband's responsibility to make sure my cup is full or overflowing. It is not even my responsibility. It is God's. Somehow He keeps pouring into my cup. He just does. I have found Him to be faithful."

"So is your cup always full?"

"No, not always full, but never empty. It's like a marriage. You need to spend time together to impact each other and have your cup filled. With God it's no different. You have to spend time with Him. Our road has been hard to walk, but God has proven Himself. At each step, He has given us encouragement and joy when there was no reason for it. His promises have been found true. I don't understand exactly how it all works, but I receive it from Him anyway. God promises to never leave us. Never. Our situation has given us the unique opportunity to see this first hand. He doesn't leave us. We know God is true."

"That's very interesting. Often, we counselors discourage people from their faith because they use it as a crutch. People think 'God loves me. God will never allow my husband to go to jail. God would never allow that!'"

I sighed and nodded. "The problem there is not the religion. The problem is that people don't always understand what is and isn't promised. God did not promise to keep us from unjust treatment. Look at Joseph. What about David in the caves? Job? The prophets? The martyrs in Hebrews? The Bible is filled with those who have been unfairly treated. And then there's Jesus. He was the most unjustly treated of all mankind and God allowed it. The Bible never promised life will be fair. As a matter-of-fact, many times it states that life will not be fair, especially for Christians. So the promise isn't that life will be fair. The promise is that He will be with us. Filling us, pouring into us, even causing us to overflow at times as He walks with us. God will never give us anything we cannot handle. He enables us whenever we walk with Him."

~ ~ ~ ~ ~ ~ ~

Back in the waiting room — the same room where I waited for Tim to be released on bail almost a year earlier. This time I waited to visit him and came home alone. The way has been brutal. Life has not been fair. God never promised it would be, but He promises to be with us. This may sound lame to some,

119

but to me it is life giving. He will never leave me nor forsake me. He will never give me more than I can handle. What then am I afraid of? He will either take the trial away or enable me to walk through it. I am not strong, but God can take the weak things and confound the wise.

Our story is filled with injustice, scare tactics, interrogations, threats and agreements others have broken. This drama is permeated with unfairness, selfishness and greed. But interwoven within this story, is another one: a story of miracles, provisions, truth revelation, broken bondages. It gushes with grace, encouragement, joy, and deeper walks with God. For everything that came against us, God had already provided a way through.

God is using this portion of our lives to purify us. To eliminate all that was not His so that we can fully commit to Him. I don't like the process, but the result is beautiful. He has given us a blanket of peace. We know the love of Christ. The assurance rests deep within us now. Tim has gotten his desire fulfilled. He ministers to fellow inmates. I don't always understand why God does things the way He does, but I don't have to understand. All I need to do is trust the One that does understand.

When things are impossible to handle, when you start dying inside, when you cannot do it on your own; look up. Look up and keep your eyes on Him. God will move. He promises. When times are tough we can expectantly wait for His Spirit to guide us. Trust Him. Lean on Him. Acknowledge Him. He promises to direct you and He has been found faithful.

At times, we felt as if a huge, looming mountain towered over us, ready to pummel us. Other times, it seemed the ground in front of us was vapor. But as we took each step, He planted solid rock under our feet. We walk on like those absurd cartoon characters that walk off a cliff into thin air. They are oblivious to their peril, but we are not. We know a huge cavern is below us. But we rejoice and look up knowing that His faithfulness will continue. He fills us, encourages us, strengthens us, and puts hope into a hopeless situation. Look to Him and He will do it for you too. He promises. He will either take the trial away or enable you to walk through it. He promises. Keep your eyes on Him. Spend time with Him. He will hide you in the shelter of the Most High.

But in all these things we overwhelmingly conquer through Him who loved us. For I am convinced that neither death, nor life, nor angels, nor principalities, nor things present, nor things to come, nor powers, nor height, nor depth, nor any other created thing, shall be able to separate us from the love of God, which is in Christ Jesus our Lord.

~ Romans 8:37-39

Incarceration of Juveniles
By Veronica A. Grabill

Colorful autumn leaves clung to the tress. The wind struggled to pull them off the branches, as I read the morning newspaper at my kitchen table. I came across a plea seeking mentors for incarcerated youth. I glanced across the room and looked at the innocent faces of my children.

As a mother of four, sadness overtook me as I thought about how traumatic for a mother to lose a child to incarceration. My maternal instinct ignited and, having completed a chaplain internship at an area hospital, I was compelled to give back to the community.

I contacted the director at the County Juvenile Detention Center and processed through the paperwork and background check. Once everything was in order, they matched me with a young, female inmate, Haley. Our first meeting was quite bazaar to say the least.

After our initial greetings and brief conversation, Haley said, "I don't like women and I worship the devil."

This is one tough young lady. I didn't know how to respond after her disclaimer. Helpless, I left the center. "God, show me how to love Haley right where she is. You didn't give up on me and I don't want to give up on her."

I was scheduled to visit with her one hour a week. The visits challenged me as Haley tried everything in her power to put up a wall. She shared the bad things that her fellow inmates had done and what she might try when she got out. I wondered if the prison system was rehabilitating these children or were they learning more tricks of the trade. I realized that her statements were made to shock me. In the eighth grade, she was failing school, running away from home, sleeping around, getting high, drinking and stealing to name a few of the offenses. In spite of her past, God allowed me to see her for who she was, a fourteen-year-old girl.

Haley was a victim of her surroundings. Her parents were divorced — her mother in jail and her father absent for years — so she lived with her Grandmother. Her rebellious and wild behavior wore out her Grandmother.

A few visits in, Haley let her guard down. She spoke freely about her behavior and feelings. I learned that the root of her hatred for women stemmed from her mother's inattentiveness toward her. My heart broke as Haley shared about her lack of direction in life. The adults in her life had failed her so she cried out for attention, even if it was negative. She came and went as she pleased and hung out with the wrong crowd just to be accepted. So many young people fall through the cracks and flirt with disaster looking for love and acceptance.

It saddened me when the governor announced that $8.4 million would be awarded to the State of Ohio capital funds for the construction of a new juvenile detention center. What a shame. If only we could strengthen the family unit and find more people to pour into the lives of our youth, then maybe this multi-million-dollar facility would not be needed.

I decided to be a part of Haley's life and introduced her to what I considered a "normal family." After displaying good behavior, she had opportunities to get a day pass from the detention center. On those days, Haley came home with me and interacted with our family. The same age as one of my daughters, it was sad to think of all that she had experienced.

My kids welcomed Haley into their world. We went to concerts, out to eat, watched movies and just hung out. She even attended church with us a few times.

After Haley's release from the detention center, we continued to visit and keep in touch. I wish I could say that all is well with her, but she resorted back to her old ways. She got into more trouble and has been in and out of the detention center several times. Now eighteen, she just had a baby by an older man.

If we want our youth to be respectful, responsible and make wise choices, then we need to help them build self-confidence. My prayer is that God directs Haley's path, breaks the generational curse and allows her to live a loving, productive life.

Train a child in the way he should go and when he is old he will not turn from it.

~ Proverbs 22:6 (NIV)

A Page from My Journal
By Cathy Joulwan

January 28:

A couple hours of watching the Super Bowl with both feet submerged in a hot, bubbly, vibrating Foot Fixer. For my husband, Chaplain Charlie, it's a perfect ending to a grueling Sunday. Charlie has served as a prison chaplain in the State of Delaware for over thirty years.

Tonight is the night before Charlie's son in the Lord is to be executed. Charlie and William Henry Flamer have known a special kinship for sixteen years, ever since Charlie led him to the Lord as many years ago.

William and Charlie had been through this count down several times before, only for William to receive a last minute stay of execution. This time however, things are different. All appeals have been exhausted. Barring a miracle, we knew it would someday come to this. That didn't make it any easier to say goodbye. Nothing left to do now but wait.

It does my heart good to see Charlie attempting to relax for an hour or so. I've always known that Charlie was tough. He grew up in the ghettos of Chicago and New York. Until these past couple of weeks, I never knew how tough he was. He's my hero, always has been and always will be.

The phone rings. William needs to talk and gave Charlie a few more last minute details. They finish their conversation as they always have, saying, "I love you."

Back to the game. Oh no! Dallas is leading!

The phone rings. A member of William's family is in need of counseling.

Game time. Dallas is still winning? Maybe this isn't going to be such a relaxing evening after all.

The phone rings. It's a lady who went to school with William. She saw Chaplain Charlie's picture in the newspaper and wants to know if there is anything that can be done to save William's life.

How much more pressure can my Charlie take? I silently prayed for him. It had been a couple years since his open heart surgery and only about a year since his last heart attack. Plus he was talking on the phone with his feet in a tub of water!

<u>January 29:</u>

As I write this entry, I notice the time. It's 11:40 Monday morning. I can hear Charlie making last minute preparations to leave by noon.

Today William will spend his last day on earth with Chaplain Charlie. I'm not sure of the quality of the time they'll have considering there will be many interruptions. Charlie will be with him through his execution.

An overwhelming sense of sadness grips my heart. I know that when Charlie comes home in the wee hours of tomorrow, it will all be over. My heart aches for Charlie as he grieves and for William as I wonder what his life might have been like if only…

I find much comfort in the fact that we have a HOPE! This goodbye, sad as it is, truly is a temporary one. Although our hearts are grieving, Psalm 116:15 assures us that "Precious in the sight of the Lord is the death of His saints."

Charlie has always considered William his son. William called him "Dad" and sent Father's Day cards and remembered all holidays and special events. The bond they shared was true and deep.

Losing William tonight makes the hope and promise of Heaven even sweeter today than it was yesterday. What a day that will be!

Several years after William's execution, Chaplain Charlie also went to be with Jesus. I am sure that William Henry Flamer was one of the first to greet him as he stepped into glory!

Those who believe in Me, even though they die, will live.
~ John 11:25

Grandma's Riddles
By Meta E. Lee

Grandma wrinkled her brow and shook her head so hard it made her honey-brown curls bounce. "I give up, Donny. Tell me the answer."

"Come on, Grams."

"Beats me." She shrugged and looked puzzled. I could tell she was trying not to smile.

"Why did the chicken cross the road," I asked again.

"Got it!" She opened her eyes so wide it made them look bluer than ever.

"To count her eggs!"

"No way. That's not even funny."

"To chase the rooster?"

"Grams, our time's running out."

"Tell me the answer, Donny. Then I got one for you."

"To get to the other side. Get it? The chicken crossed the road to get to the other side."

"Everyone knows that."

"You didn't, Grams."

"Well, Mr. Five-Year-Old–Riddle-Champion, now it's my turn. Why did the fireman wear red suspenders?"

"I'm almost six. Anyhow, that riddle's old."

"Older than me, but I still need an answer." She tapped her fingers on the table. "I'm waiting."

"To hold his pants up!"

"You got it!" She always clapped when I got a riddle right. "You're sharper than a tack. Sharper than your daddy was at six."

"Let's do knock-knocks next month."

"Knock-knocks it will be." She stood and hugged me tight. "You can always ask me anything, not just riddles." Grandma rubbed her hand under her nose. She snored and sniffled at the same time. My grandma joined the line with the other ladies. She turned toward me and waved a good-bye. "You're a good boy, Donny. Stay good." She made the words with her mouth, not out loud. When the ladies started to leave the visiting room, they looked like we do in school when we go to lunch. Even though they're grown-ups, they make a real straight line.

"Bye, Grams. I'm gonna have some good knock-knocks," I called out. I don't think she heard me because everyone was yelling their goodbyes and stuff as the ladies left the room.

~ ~ ~ ~ ~ ~ ~

"Grandma," I said at our visit the next month, "I wanna ask you something. It's not exactly a riddle."

"Anything, Donny."

"Daddy says there's a baby in Mom's tummy and that the baby is gonna live with us when it's here. How come?"

"Don't look at your shoes, boy. I'm sitting right here."

"Daddy says he'll tell me more about it when I'm bigger. But this kid at school s---"

"I'll tell you, Donny. Don't know why your daddy got so silent all of a sudden."

So Grandma told me what she called the "birds and bees talk." It was funny listening to Grandma use real words for things. Real words for like how you go to the bathroom.

"Donny, when you were a little baby they brought you right here to see me. I couldn't wait until that visiting day. Your daddy said that you were a fussy baby and did lots of crying. 'No fussbudgets allowed here,' I told him. So, I held you real close, sang you a song and you gave me a great big smile. That was the first smile you gave anyone. I'll always remember that,

Donny." She did that snore-sniffle sound again. "I got your first smile."

After the "birds and the bees" we did knock-knock riddles. They made more sense to me than that other stuff. My grandma is real smart. She knew the "who's there?" before I could give the answer.

That's how it is with me and Grandma. Jokes and riddles and serious stuff too. Just before my tenth birthday, we talked serious stuff. Real serious.

"Grandma," I said in a whisper, "I'm in trouble. Everyone's mad at me. You'll be mad, too."

"I'm not mad, Don. Not yet, that is. I don't even know what you're talking about. Might as well get it out so we can do our riddles."

"There's this girl in my class and I guess I like her. Not a lot. Just like her. Her name's Tameka. When I was alone in the classroom, I went around to the other kids' desks and took pencils and markers. I tied them with rubber bands I got from the teacher's desk. I gave them to Tameka for Valentime's. Mrs. Valero found out and made me return the pencils to the other kids. I had to do it right there in front of everyone. Tameka was crying. Mrs. Valero said that no one should bring me a Valentime."

"Oh, Donny." Grandma said with a slight grimace. "You know it was wrong to take the pencils. Real wrong." She shook her head. "That must have been really embarrassing."

"I'm sorry."

"And while I am correcting you, young man, it's Valentine's Day with an 'n' not an 'm.'"

"That's not all, Grandma."

"Don't look at your shoes, boy. I'm sitting right where I always do."

"Well, Mom and Daddy got a phone call from Mrs. Valero and they both started yelling at me at once. Then Mom screamed and said that I'm gonna to grow up just like you, Grams, just like you. She said I'll end up in jail just like you. She started to cry and ran out of the room. Daddy ran after her. I was left in the kitchen with my jerky sister. We hadn't even had supper yet. We could have starved to death."

"Donny," Grandma bit her lip. This was the first time my grandma looked old. Her face got real droopy and her nose got red. "Donny, your Grandma made a mistake, you know that. You don't have to be any way you don't want to be. You're a good boy." She hugged me and made her snore-sniffle sound.

Grandma said that she was tired and left the visiting room early that day. Way before the other ladies. As she was leaving, she turned and said what she always says, "You're a good boy, Donny. Stay good."

~ ~ ~ ~ ~ ~ ~

The time I turned sixteen, I drove to see Grams by myself. My dad said that I'm a good driver so he let me borrow the car. I think he was relieved. He always seemed uneasy seeing his mother in prison. As soon as I walked into the visiting room, Grams let out a loud shriek. Almost a hoot. I thought for sure she'd set off an alarm and the guards would come over and drag her, or me, away.

"Good Lord," she shouted on the top of her lungs. "What have we here?" I couldn't tell if she was smiling or not because she slapped her hand over her mouth. "This has got to be the riddle of the week. No, this is definitely the riddle of the new millennium." Then her voice got even louder. "What is it that is over six feet tall, weighs too little, has blue hair, a diamond growing out of its left nostril and a safety pin stuck in its right eyebrow?"

131

"Grandma, not so loud."

"Don't interrupt. I'm not done yet." She took off her eyeglasses and wiped them on her skirt. "What's more, its shirt's wide open like Harry Bellefonté but the chest ain't black. What is it?"

"You know it's me."

"The only way I know it's you is that you're staring at your shoes, if you can call those raggedy sneakers, shoes." I glared at her, but she went on and on. "I'm surprised your parents let you out of the house. More surprised that they let you in here." She adjusted her eyeglasses. "You sure don't look like Donald Eric Boyd."

"This is what I am about."

"What you are about, young man, is being a wonderful kid. A boy who is smart, funny and also very special to his grandma."

"Yeah."

"Cut your hair. Let it grow brown like it's supposed to be. Give the nose diamond to a girlfriend. And," she was really shouting now, "Button that shirt!"

"Guess I'm not gonna win this one."

"No, you're not. I might be locked up but I can still say what I think. I always have and always will." She shook her head and took a deep breath. "Now young man, I have a math puzzle that will really get you thinking." We did math puzzles for a while. She never had to use no paper or pencil.

After an hour, visiting time was over. When Grams left she was laughing with the other ladies in line. Guess I didn't look all that bad.

~ ~ ~ ~ ~ ~ ~

I hoped to see Grams a couple of days after I received my college acceptance and scholarship letter. I drove to the prison on the usual visiting day. At the Sally Port, the place where visitors sign in and say their inmate's number and dormitory unit, the guard said, "She's confined to quarters."

Over the years I've learned not to ask too many questions because there'll be no answers. Later I found out that my grandmother got into a fight with another inmate and visiting privileges were revoked. This altercation, or whatever they call it, is unusual for my grandmother; she's really not like that.

I rarely thought about what my grandmother did and why she was in prison. After my dad's father passed away, she got kind of crazy and married an awful guy. It was about drinking and domestic homicide. "The past," according to Grandma, "has been left behind. Every new day has something to offer. I make the best of it." My grandmother has always made the best of her situation.

~ ~ ~ ~ ~ ~ ~

During winter vacation of my senior year of college, the usually drab visiting room was decorated with paper cutouts for Christmas, Chanukah and Kwanzaa too. It's kind of ironic seeing snowmen and snowflakes in Florida.

"Glad you're here, boy." Grams grabbed hold of my hand. It was like being held by a rag doll so flimsy and floppy. We walked to the Christmas tree in the corner of the room. Grams reached out, her hand shook a lot, and stroked one of the branches.

"Smell this, Donny. It's a real Christmas tree. A real one. First Christmas tree I've seen in years. Fifteen or twenty, I lose track. Smell it. It's wonderful!"

I cleared my throat. "Now, I have something wonderful for you."

"College riddles? Nothing too dirty I hope. Couldn't take it!"

"No riddles just good news; great news." I told Grams about my girlfriend, Michelle. "We're getting married after graduation!"

Grandma stood there, shook her head and did her snore-sniffle routine. She swayed a little, grabbed the back of a straight back chair and sat down. "Oh, Donny, my little Donny." Grams looked up at me and then down at her hands. Slowly she pulled a gold band from the ring finger of her right hand. "This is for you. For your girl," she whispered.

"No way, Grams. It's yours. Your only jewelry."

"No more, Donny. It's yours now. Anyways, it's too big. I had to wrap masking tape around it."

I protested.

"Donald Eric Boyd, your old grandma can be tough, very tough. You better do what I say." She made a motion like she was holding a gun. "You give this ring to your Michelle."

"I call her Shelly."

"Tell Shelly it's from me." Grandma lined up with the other ladies. Her walk was more like a shuffle. Before she left the room, she leaned against the wall and turned toward me. "You're a good boy, Donny. Stay good."

I loved my grandmother more that day than at any other time.

~ ~ ~ ~ ~ ~ ~

The day of my most important riddle the weather was cold. The heat didn't work in the visiting room and everyone; visitors, inmates and guards, grumbled. Nobody fixed it. My breath lingered in the air like rain clouds.

I couldn't find Grandma right away. Tandra, one of her roommates, pointed to the corner of the room. She was slumped over in her wheelchair.

"Grams," I nudged her foot with mine. "Grams," I repeated even louder. "I have the best riddle ever."

"What? Oh, it's you, Donny. How come…"

"Grams, wake up."

"I am awake."

"I have the best riddle ever." I'm sure I was grinning. "What is bald as a billiard ball, has no teeth, has skin as soft as rose petals, has wet pants and wants to meet her great-grandmother?" I pulled back my little daughter's pink blanket and set the baby right on top of Grandma's lap without letting go.

"Oh, Donny. No one told me."

"Now it's time for you to get to know your great-granddaughter." Just then the baby squirmed and cried.

"No fussbudgets allowed here, little lady." Grandma held the baby by herself. She sang a song I never heard her sing before. To me, it sounded like an angel singing. My baby stopped crying, stared at her great-grandmother and smiled.

"What a smile." Grandma smiled back. "She's beautiful, Donny. Beautiful."

"Guess what her name is."

"How am I supposed to know?"

"Grandma she is named after you, Judith Thelma Boyd."

"She got my name?" Grandma shook her head so hard, her sparse gray curls bounced around. "My name."

All three of us, Grandma, me and little Judith Thelma made that snore-sniffle sound. We cried together.

Valerie L. Coleman

The Joy of the Lord is My Strength
By Joy Marino

The Spirit of the Lord GOD is upon me; because the Lord hath anointed me to preach good tidings unto the meek; He hath sent me to bind up the brokenhearted, to proclaim liberty to the captives, and the opening of the prison to them that are bound; To proclaim the acceptable year of the Lord, and the day of vengeance of our God; to comfort all that mourn; To appoint unto them that mourn in Zion, to give unto them beauty for ashes, the oil of joy for mourning, the garment of praise for the spirit of heaviness; that they might be called trees of righteousness, the planting of the Lord, that He might be glorified.
~ Isaiah 61:1-3

Overwhelmed by a series of events, my body went limp and crashed to the floor. Unable to endure anymore pain, I succumbed to depression.

In 1996 I had a miscarriage. By 1997, I had my first daughter, Talia, and then gained about twenty pounds. In addition to postpartum depression, my self-esteem was damaged. My grandmother died from diabetic complications in 1998. Her death was difficult for me because she was so much more than just my grandmother. She was a mighty prayer warrior who embodied the Proverb 31 woman. She encouraged me and believed God to do a mighty work in my life. She taught me the meaning of unconditional love. I thank God for the time He allowed her to be in my life. "To everything there is a season."

In 2001, I released some of my pain because God had blessed my family with new life. This pregnancy gave me hope for tomorrow, but it wasn't long before the enemy attacked. I was eight months pregnant, when Talia was diagnosed as having a trichobezoar in her stomach. The mass extended nine inches into her intestines. A trichobezoar, which is generally found in cats, is a hairball that is mixed in with food and particles. The result of a rare condition where people pull out their hair and eat it, a trichobezoar can infect the blood which is extremely dangerous and often fatal.

My daughter had stopped eating. My husband and I had to force her to consume each meal and then she vomited. We had taken her to several different doctors and they all diagnosed her as anorexic. We challenged this diagnosis and continued to seek help. My daughter's pediatrician decided to examine her stomach and sent her to the Children's Hospital for x-rays. In preparation for the x-rays, a nurse gave Talia a solution to drink. The liquid was supposed to pass through her digestive tract, but hours later it did not. The doctors looked closer at the x-ray and found a large mass, a trichobezoar.

My daughter had surgery to remove the trichobezoar. We were in the hospital for almost two weeks. Not more than two months had passed before she was diagnosed with another one. The doctors said that she was eating her hair as a result of depression, but I knew otherwise. My child was not depressed. She was under attack by a demonic spirit. I prayed and had my church in prayer for her, until God revealed to me what I had to do. He showed me the Scripture in the Bible about the little girl who was possessed and how it was by her mother's faith that she was made whole. I felt something stir in the pit of my soul. God was not going to allow me to stay depressed. I had to come out. I had to believe.

The night before the second surgery, Talia told me that Jesus healed her. She described a dream in which He pulled this mass out of her body. Remember, she was four years old. Convinced, I called her surgeon.

"Doctor, my daughter no longer needs surgery. The Lord healed her."

"Oh, really? And just how did this healing take place?"

"She told me that He removed it in her dream."

"Mrs. Marino, I know that you are overwhelmed with your daughter's condition and the new baby, however that's just not possible. Did she vomit or pass it in her stool?"

"No, she ju---"

"Well, we'll continue with the surgery as planned. I'll see you in the morning. Get some rest. We have a long day ahead of us."

I prayed and decided to continue with the surgery scheduled for October 31, 2002. God set us up to get His glory.

Right before the anesthesiologist administered the anesthesia, my daughter told everyone in the operating room that Jesus had already healed her. They laughed and wrote her off as an adorable, creative, little girl who was probably a bit high from sedation. They put her under and began the surgery. Within minutes they woke her up and said that they could not find a mass. In complete disbelief, they sent for her x-rays thinking maybe they had mixed up the patients. The mass showed up on the x-ray, but not inside her body. Praise God! Some refused to accept the miracle, while others were baffled by God's work.

Talia was completely healed, but by November my uncle was diagnosed with colon cancer. He lived almost two months to the day of his diagnosis and then died in January 2003. Later that year, I lost another uncle to liver failure. I was furious, but not with God. He had done too much for me to continue with the pathetic pity parties. Although God did not heal my uncles,

He is still a healer! Whenever doubt tried to overpower me, I just looked at Talia!

Convinced that my God was a healer the enemy redirected his attention to me. In March 2004, I was diagnosed with fibroid tumors. My abdomen had swollen to the size of a five-month-pregnant woman. My doctors demanded I have surgery as soon as possible and used scare tactics to convince me. I knew God did not give us the spirit of fear and I knew He told me to be anxious for nothing, but I was afraid. I forgot who He called me to be and the ministry, visions, and dreams that were still ahead of me. I then remembered that the work God began in me had to be completed because He said it and He cannot lie. I had the surgery and to the surgeons' surprise I did not have fibroids. I had uterine and endometrial polyps. They removed all but one polyp. According to the doctors, if they removed the remaining lump, I might bleed to death because it was embedded in my endometrial lining. When I went in for my post-surgery annual check up, the polyp no longer existed. Praise God!

In 2006 I was attacked again but this time they tried to scare me with the notion that I might have endometrial cancer. Victory, yet again! The enemy did not stop the attacks. The difference was that I had learned how to stand on the Word of God.

Just recently I underwent a series of diagnostic tests for breast cancer. After two months of agony, I received a letter on Saturday, April 14, 2007 indicating that my left breast was completely normal. Gloraaaaaay to God! The culmination of life-threatening experiences drained me and caused my knees to buckle. But by his unmerited favor, I went from faint and paralyzed to strong and resilient in His Word. When the finisher of my faith completed His work, the devil was, is and always will be a liar. I did not have, do not have, and will not ever have any form of cancer in my body. Because I am saved I am healed. I stand whole in Him. Thank You, Jesus!

So here I am in 2007, the year of completion. God told me that it is time for this season and everything in it to end so He can begin or birth something new in me. I am dying to self to allow more room for God. He increases my faith daily and I am walking closer to Him. God is calling me to a new level. My obedience will propel me into my destiny. Everything I endured was preparation for the work God has called me to do. My hurt, pain, heartache and depression were never about me, but a testimony of what God can do. The joy of the Lord is my strength. I was called to the nations for such a time as this!

These things I have spoken unto you, that in Me you might have peace. In the world you will have tribulation: but be of good cheer; I have overcome the world.
~ John 16:33

Searching for Home
By Amanda C. Bauch

My freshman year of college, I walked into my dorm room after dinner with friends. Allison, my roommate, was in the library studying, as usual. I was grateful to be alone. I leaned against the door. Something was missing, a void that may never be filled. I felt destined to spend my life with this sense of worthlessness, and I had no one to blame but myself. As the first person in my family to go to college, I could have used the opportunity to better myself, to try to figure out why I acted the way I did. When I seemed to make progress toward happiness and fulfillment, why did I hit the self-destruct button? Was I too proud to ask for help, or simply too afraid?

As if in a trance, I walked to my desk and riffled around in the drawer. I grabbed my bottled water and opened the container of pain killers which I kept handy for menstrual cramps. I dumped the pills onto the desk. They rolled around with their shiny surfaces reflecting the light from my banker's lamp.

I took one pill and swallowed it, then another and another. I mechanically swallowed most of the pills; how many I don't know. My mind refused to acknowledge what I was doing. I was only going to nap, that's all. Just like I usually did after dinner.

I climbed onto the top bunk and went to sleep. I wish I could say that something romantic happened during that time, something profoundly spiritual: angels, a bright white light at the end of a tunnel, or some other proverbial near-death experience. All I experienced was darkness, a stillness I'd never felt before. Actually, I'm not even sure about the darkness. I assume it must have been darkness, for wouldn't I have emerged from my drugged stupor to relate my glorious tale to others, had it been a time filled with light, love and evidence of the hereafter?

Instead, I awoke to a light that pierced my corneas. My eyes closed to block out the sunlight. After a few moments of adjustment, I opened them to a squint. The sunlight angled through the blinds so it shone in diagonal stripes along my body. I heard faint sounds of people walking in the hallway, going up and down the stairs, in and out of the bathroom across the hall.

Is Allison here? I slowly lifted my head, which felt filled with wet concrete, turned slightly, and saw she wasn't. I fell back against the pillows to ease some of the throbbing pain. Allison probably wouldn't have questioned my sleep marathon anyway, as I was prone to taking to my bed for entire days. It wouldn't have seemed out of the ordinary. And none of my professors would have thought to alert anyone either — to them I was nothing more than an empty chair in class. My mind was removed from time, my throat and mouth parched. I tried to say my name, but it came out as a croak.

I didn't know how many days had passed while the world continued on without me consciously in it, how many times people had walked past my room, chatting and carrying on the day's business.

The tears pooled in my ears and overflowed onto my stale-smelling pillow. I couldn't even kill myself successfully.

~ ~ ~ ~ ~ ~ ~

Five years and three colleges later, I found myself slipping again. The second semester at my new school didn't go as well as the first. I had accepted the position of chief copy editor of the college's weekly newspaper, which entailed more responsibility than I had anticipated. I despaired when my grades dropped, and I missed classes because I wasn't getting enough sleep. Things got so bad that some of my professors asked me if everything was all right. They'd had me the previous semester and knew I was capable of better work. My friends also encouraged me to quit the paper because they could see I was unhappy. However, they didn't know how bad things truly were. A new bout of depression had begun. If I hadn't filled my schedule with class, the paper, or the dining hall, my days would have been spent curled under my bed covers, hiding from the world. I fought to stay positive and motivated, increasingly difficult as the long, cold winter days wore on. Thoughts of suicide drifted through my consciousness.

That night at the paper I asked our advisor if I could meet with him. We went into his office.

"What's going on?"

"I need to resign my position at the paper."

"Well, you know that if you do, you won't be able to come back and work for us again, whether it's as a work-study student or a volunteer."

"Yes, I know, but..." I paused, unsure about how much I should tell him. I didn't want him to think I was nuts, but my pride and professionalism didn't want him to think I was a quitter either. "Look, here's the situation. I've been struggling with depression for most of my life, and once," I took a deep breath. "Once I even tried to kill myself." He leaned back in his chair and steepled his fingers in front of his mouth. I wasn't sure if he didn't know how to respond, or if he just figured it was better to listen. I continued. "You know I love the work I do here, but I've been feeling really down lately. I've been

143

scared about what will happen if I carry on this way. It's just not healthy for me to be here right now."

"Well, I can understand that. And considering your situation, I wouldn't have a problem with you coming in to help out every so often."

"Thank you," I said as I stood. "Long night tonight to get the paper ready to go to press, right?"

The night ended up being even longer than I expected. We had a rare emergency meeting with the senior staff and our advisor. A girl threw herself out her third-floor dorm window, got caught by her shirt, and hung there, screaming for help. Someone walking by saw her fall to the ground and called campus safety. She was taken to the hospital, and no one knew her condition.

We deliberated for what seemed like forever — who would write the article, whether it would be the lead article, and what details would be included. The girl who claimed authorship of the article for herself, someone I considered a snob — the type who would backstab whoever she needed to make it big — demanded that the girl's name be printed.

"Come on," she said, "she had to know when she threw herself out her window that everyone was going to know her name. As the source for campus news, we should be the first to tell everyone who it was."

I'd been silent until that moment. "I highly doubt that poor girl was thinking, 'Oh no, I'd better not try to kill myself because my name will be in the paper.' You people are a freakin' joke. You know that?" I ran out of the room before I embarrassed myself by breaking down.

The advisor found me sitting on the floor at the end of the hall a few minutes later. He touched my shoulder. "We're not printing the name."

I thanked him through my tears.

"Whenever you're ready, you should go home. You've had enough for one day."

When I got back to my dorm room, some of the girls on my floor had decorated my door with congratulatory signs. One friend had made a poster on her computer, with a picture of a newspaper roasting over a fire. My other neighbor had written a poem on a long scroll telling how proud she was of me. For the second time that night I cried, but this time it was in gratitude for the wonderful people that looked out for me.

That weekend, I bought enough alcohol to host a small party in my single dorm room. I'd never been drunk before. And this was the first night I actually wanted to get drunk, to be completely oblivious.

Although I passed out long before the party ended, I was awakened early in the morning by Jules, delicately removing my clothing to put me to bed. Jules rarely got drunk, so she was often left to help those who were unable to find their way to bedrooms or bathrooms.

In my sleepy-drunken stupor, I revealed myself to her. I told her the dark things I kept hidden inside: the abuse, Pa's death, Ma's alcoholism, my suicide attempt. She sat on the bed next to me and listened in silence.

I also told her about some of what kept me going, particularly my love for my sister and my great-grandmother. I told Jules about my guilt when Great-Gram had a stroke and ended up in a nursing home. I explained how it was hard to see her, usually so full of life and energy, bound in a wheelchair and unable to even do her crossword puzzles. As the sun rose, I mentioned my constant concern over the woman whose name I bore, who always made me feel valuable and precious.

I awoke a couple of hours later to the phone ringing. *Who is calling me at eight on a Saturday morning?* I almost let it go to voicemail, but somehow knew I should answer it.

"Hello?"

"Mandy, it's Jada." My sister's words sounded strained. Her tone concerned and alerted me. Something was wrong. And when something was wrong in my family, that meant someone was dead.

"It's Great-Gram... Mandy, she died about five this morning."

"How? What happened?"

"In her sleep. The nurses at the home were there."

I didn't respond.

"Frank and I are coming to get you today. We should be there sometime in the afternoon."

"Okay."

"Hang in there, kiddo."

I hung up the phone. Numb. Like an automaton, I stood, opened my door and walked to Jules and Kate's dorm room. I knocked and walked in. They were both still in bed and sat up when I entered. Looking at Jules with wide, disbelieving eyes, I said, "Great-Gram is dead."

The ride home was a surreal nightmare of winter weather. Visibility was so low we could hardly see the taillights of the car just a few feet ahead. As darkness fell, it got even worse. A number of cars parked on the road's shoulder, emergency lights flashing in futility, tractor trailers jackknifed into ditches and medians.

When I felt insecure during road trips, I slept. I figured that way I wouldn't see the end coming. Of course, it was impossible for me to sleep on this trip. I listened to Jules's mix tape over and over again, trying to memorize the lyrics, searching for hope and inspiration in them. Once in awhile I cried. Jada gave me concerned glances from the front seat, but I shook my head at her. She knew there was nothing she could do. I would deal with things my own way.

We managed to arrive in Falconer without incident. Ma wasn't home.

"Are you sure you want to be alone," Jada asked.

"I'll be fine. I'm going right to bed anyway." I climbed in the fold-out futon and hugged my black cat for comfort. The words of James Taylor's *You've Got a Friend* on the mix tape lulled me to sleep. "You just call out my name, and you know wherever I am..."

Like most families, only two occasions drew us together — weddings and funerals. Despite the horrible weather, all of the cousins and old friends flocked to the service. My immediate family and I had been there so many times over the years that we were on a familiar, first-name basis with the funeral home owner and director.

A female pastor gave the service, in calm, soothing tones. We were comforted by her reassuring words of salvation and eternal life.

After being introduced by the pastor, I stood behind the podium, took a deep breath to calm my nerves, prayed for strength and then began. I opened with a reading from I Peter 1:6-7: "'In this you greatly rejoice, though now for a little while you may have had to suffer grief in all kinds of trials. These have come so that your faith — of greater worth than gold, which perishes even though refined by fire — may be proved genuine and may result in praise, glory and honor.'"

I tried to elicit memories of happier times, like when the extended family spent Thanksgiving together. But I mostly talked about Great-Gram as a person: the notorious packrat she was, her bottomless breadbox of cookies and her rocking chair. I'd never been a fan of eulogies that only gave glowing recollections of the deceased; everyone has flaws. So I also mentioned how Granny was obstinate and opinionated, loved her *Bring on the Rotten Cat!* poem and said things like "They think their stuff don't stink!"

I closed with a poem by Emily Brontë, *No Coward Soul Is Mine*. The even, balanced verses provided the same comfort as I'd had as a little girl, sitting on Great-Gram's lap.

The rest of my time in Falconer was spent sorting through what was left of Great-Gram's belongings and saying goodbye to all the relatives who'd come for the funeral. The night before I returned to school, I thought about my state of mind, and all the recurring issues I'd had with depression. I had a problem, and it was about time I did something about it. The way I saw it, I had two options: deal with my illness the wrong way — with alcohol, drugs, or some other form of self-destruction or deal with my illness the right way, the healthy way. When I got back to school, I committed myself to counseling and even to taking antidepressants if necessary.

My trip for the funeral had shown me that Falconer was no longer a solution. I recalled the times when it had been a refuge for me, a welcome release from Oklahoma and New York City. But I acknowledged that the only reason Falconer had appealed to me then was because it seemed to present a better alternative, not because I genuinely wanted to be there. When I lived in an apartment with no heat, water, or electricity, almost anything was an improvement. Although Falconer might have been able to provide the physical comfort and familiarity I craved during those times, it never gave me the emotional and mental solace I needed.

Over the years I had managed to convince myself that if I just found the perfect place to live, then I would at last be all right. But no matter how many times I moved, I never seemed to find what I sought — happiness, inner peace and a place to call home. I realized that home wasn't a specific geographic location. Home was the place where I would come to terms with myself. I had tried to find the answers, a search that took me halfway across the country and back, but of course the answers were in the last place I thought to look — inside myself.

As Jada and Frank drove me back to college the next day, I remembered the words of Brontë's poem[1]:

"No coward soul is mine

No trembler in the world's storm-troubled sphere

I see Heaven's glories shine

And Faith shines equal arming me from Fear"

It would feel good to be home.

[1]The publisher's information for Brontë's poem is available at http://Academic.Brooklyn.cuny.edu/english/melani/novel_19c/wuthering/poetry.html.

Refilled, Renewed
By Larry Sells

Lamppost, a Christian coffee shop and theatre, opened the summer of 2003 in Cedar Falls, Iowa. I walked in and glanced at the multicolored floor squares. I enjoyed the warm atmosphere and took a seat. According to the wall menu, they served a variety of coffees, hot chocolate, and smoothies. I ordered a mocha latte and Chuck, a volunteer, made it in a few minutes. I tasted it and loved the way the whip cream and chocolate looked like a spider web. While I sat and sipped, Chuck and I talked about events at other local coffee shops.

"We plan to hold poetry readings, theatre plays and live music in the theatre part of the building." Chuck said as he pointed to the door leading into the back.

I accepted his invitation to walk through the door. The last time I had entered the building it was a funeral home. In place of wooden pews and a pulpit were a stage, lights, chairs, tables and a couple of booths. They had transformed it from a place for the dead into a place for the living.

That fall, the Lamppost put on its first play, *The Wedding.* I missed it because I had to wash dishes at Carlos O'Kelly's restaurant. I learned that the Lamppost was designed as a Christian meeting place. At that time, I did not have a good relationship with God. When I visited, I lied to people who asked me if I was a Christian. Life had used me up and I just wanted to be left alone to enjoy my latte. I returned month after month and they accepted me as I was — a non-Christian.

July 2004, I had a relapse of my depression. I was admitted to the mental ward of Covenant in Waterloo, Iowa. A month prior, I was taken off Thioridazine and put on a low dose of Seroquel, apparently insufficient to offset my stress level. The change in medicine triggered my bout of depression and anxiety.

Two weeks later, the Seroquel level was adequate for me to be released. On the way home, I had my landlord, El Jean Bartelt, stop at Lamppost, so I could have a mocha latte. *I have tried everything except turning to Christ and God*, I thought. Afterwards, El Jean dropped me off at home and then drove across the street to park in her driveway.

I found my *Life Application Bible*, which was given to me by a friend. I turned to John 3:16. "'For God loved the world so much that He gave His only Son so that anyone who believes in Him shall not perish but have eternal life.'" I closed the Bible and prayed. "Christ, I believe in You with my entire heart. Please take away my sins and replace them with Your blood from the cross. Enter my heart so You can guide me from my darkness to the light of forgiveness and life."

A few days later, I attended Lampost's Bible study group. I was invited to attend the church service at First Baptist Church at the corner of Main and Seventh Streets. John Fuller, the pastor, talked about accountability. I realized that I am only accountable for myself to God. I'm not accountable for what my father did to me. In fact, I had to forgive him and let Christ have the driver's seat of my life.

During the closing prayer, I made my request known. "God, help me forgive my father for the things he did out of anger." The burden of decades of guilt and hate lifted off my shoulders. "Lord, You are the center of my life and I'm going to do my best to serve You."

I told Pastor Fuller that the sermon helped me to find peace in Christ. My heart and my soul warmed to the idea that I would never be alone again because Christ would be with me through eternity.

In September 2004, I attended a men's Bible study group which met on Monday nights. We studied the book of John with the *Life Application Workbook.* My soul ate up the Word of God, and I grew as a Christian.

During one of the early meetings, I confessed that I felt like I was constantly falling short of God's expectations. The other members of the study group explained that Christ helps Christians meet God's expectations. He rose from the grave so that we could have a solid and loving relationship with God, the Father.

At the next meeting, Dave Hughes brought me a book. *Grace Walk* helped me to understand that God wanted me to have a closer relationship with Him. So as I grew as a Christian, I became closer to Him.

By the end of spring, the men's Bible study finished the book of John. We agreed to break for the summer and start with a new book in the fall. My spiritual growth did not stop as I continued to read the Word with four devotional books.

On April 30, 2005, I was returning from Des Moines when I felt a mental tug as I passed a sign that read "Faith Baptist Bible College in Ankeny, IA." I knew that I needed to apply to the college to increase my knowledge of the Bible. My spiritual life continued to develop, and I felt renewed.

I wrote Christian articles, poetry with a religious slant and personal essays that dealt with my faith and mental illness. Studying the Bible and writing fed my soul. When the new ideas and topics entered by mind, I felt refilled and recharged.

Pastor Chris preached that as believers we should step up and increase our level of participation of faith. This sermon caused me to apply to Faith Baptist Bible College. I returned to Des Moines that Wednesday to check on low-income housing. I was informed that I needed to apply at Des Moines Housing

Authority (DMHA) to get on a waiting list. DMHA could not guarantee me an apartment and with the high price of fuel, I canceled my move.

On June 26, 2005, I was one of forty-five people baptized by immersion. While I was backstage waiting for my turn, I prayed.

"Lord, please don't let me lose my pants." They were the slip-on variety. "And Father, let my mother watch me from Heaven."

At my turn to be baptized, I inched into the huge white tub and sat on a white bucket seat. It looked like one of those hot tubs owned by rich people. Pastor Jason reminded me to sit back so they could lean me into the water. With my mouth and nose covered by a dry handkerchief, they dipped me into the cool water and returned me to a sitting position. Pastor Justin and a helper assisted me out of the baptismal tub as Pastor Chris tossed me a dry towel. I caught it with one hand and then realized that my pants still covered everything that they were supposed to. *Thank You, Lord.*

I'm still reading the Bible and I'm looking at taking computer Bible courses. I'm disappointed about not moving to Des Moines, but Christ knows how I'm going to serve Him. This realization refreshes me as I wait. Who would have thought that a cup of mocha latte would usher me to the Lord?

Breaking Free from Obesity's Stronghold
By Erin Di Paolo

Holly is one of my best friends. She is also fat. That makes Holly my fat friend. How fat is she? She is seventy pounds overweight. How does she feel about being obese? She loathes it. How did she get that way? It's a long story. What will it take for her to change? That is yet to be seen.

In her own words, Holly is fat, lazy, ugly and unfeeling. She is angry — at herself, at God and at the person who is indirectly responsible for her being fat. Her older brother, Jeff, who was supposed to nurture and protect her, instead sexually abused her, years ago, when they were both young, innocent children. Their innocence vanished and in an instant, everything changed for both of them. Holly bares the scars, most visible in her obese, self-destructive body. I am sure her brother bares scares, too. If not, he should.

Holly said her brother used "dirty phrases" during his manipulation and exploitation of her. One of his favorites was "Mommy's gone." When Holly heard that phrase, she became petrified. He threatened her with this phrase, over and over, trying to will her into compliance. It worked. He said these words not so much during the physical abuse, but as a way to emotionally abuse Holly; to get her into a submission mindset. My fat friend has never recovered.

"Does it hurt?" was another phrase Holly's brother said to her. She remembers lying on her mother's bed, with her brother groping her and asking the question. Holly's crumpled heart does not allow her to remember further details. Though it did not hurt, Holly lied and told her brother it did. She clung to the hope that it would prompt him to stop the behavior. Even in her young, vulnerable state, my friend was smart. She knew in her soul that something was terribly wrong about his actions, but she was powerless to change them. She remains so today, though the abuse has long since ceased. The abuse she inflicts on her soul and body remains relentless in their pursuit of her. Will they ultimately win?

During the abuse, Holly stared, mindlessly, at the television set. If she could escape into that imaginary land, becoming one with the television, then everything would be all right. At least that is the lie she told herself. The lie continues to this day. My precious fat friend persists in using the endless drone of the television set to escape the horror of her past and the horror of the days she still experiences. The agony requires more diversion each time, forcing her to watch more and more TV.

If only TV were her lone escape. She eats, too. Eats and eats and eats, trying unsuccessfully to block out the memories. She smokes. One puff after the next helps her forget. These things enable her to temporarily disengage from the past, from the present, from the future. But none of them will ever give her the fulfillment, love and acceptance she so desperately needs.

Holly, my tall, beautiful, brown-haired friend, has become her own abuser. She numbs herself with countless hours of mindless TV and tons of food, simply to avoid reality. And she is killing herself slowly by smoking one cigarette after the next, hoping for sweet relief. Relief never comes.

While Holly was the innocent, sweet little child in this case, she endured it alone. "Where was God," she asked herself. And where were her parents? After her brother abused her the first time, she went to her parents and told them everything. Can you imagine what strength that took for a little girl who had been violated at the hands of her older brother?

She summoned up the courage, with her brother in the same room, to show her parents what he did. Her father looked at him and asked why he did it. Holly does not remember Jeff's response, if he had one, and then the entire subject was dropped. Just like that. Holly once again was left alone with her abuse, with no one to run to, no where to go. It angers me to think that nothing was done to rescue this desperate, aching, devastated young girl. Was there anyone she could trust? Apparently not.

Twenty years later, Holly brought the situation up again to her parents. Her mother denied ever hearing about it and her father looked at her, shocked, and said, "I had no idea you remembered." As if she could ever forget. With responses like that, is it any wonder Holly drowns her sorrow with TV, food, and cigarettes? If it were me, I would probably throw in drugs and alcohol, if the truth be told.

During another abuse situation, Holly recalled her brother encouraged her to "Just touch it." Fearful of what he would do if she didn't, she obeyed. Thank God that's as far as it went or at least that is all she recalls. Either way, a terrible injustice was committed against her. And not by a stranger, but by evil incarnate, masquerading as a brother. Despicable.

I'm sure Jeff has his own unique ways of avoiding the darkness of his soul, even today. Holly does not have the luxury. Her abuse is with her, always haunting her, in the form of the latest reality television show, a bag of cookies or a pack of cigarettes. All she has to do is reach out and grab the comfort, just like her brother had her reach for him so many years ago. But now, like then, comfort is elusive. A delay of the inevitable; the excruciating process of someday coming to terms with all that happened, all that was taken, and all that was lost.

Holly remembered that her brother told her to "Take your clothes off." One warm, summer day, she swam with her brother in their plastic alligator pool. Who doesn't think back on sunny, idyllic days spent swimming with siblings? Not a care in the world. Only swimming with Jeff was not heart-warming. When Holly swam with her brother, bad things happened. After their swim, he called her upstairs and told her to remove her clothes. He had a sensual quality about his voice, like the lilting voice of Marilyn Monroe in one of her movies or a would-be lover, swooning over the object of his affection. She followed his demand, but recalled no other details. The words still echo in her ears, haunting her.

Similar situations have happened with other significant people in her life. Most people don't understand, like the friend who recently shared a pizza with Holly. After reading what Holly had written about her abuse, the friend declared it disturbing. She urged Holly to not share the information with another living soul. What's really disturbing is that a young woman with so much to offer has the abuse repeated by others, only in different ways.

What is the answer for my friend who is a wonderful wife, mother, photographer and friend? Will she ever be able to do more than she does right now, which is simply survive? Holly realizes, as we all do, that survival is not living. It is far from it.

Not only does Holly allow toxic things into her body, she refuses to let what is non-toxic — her tears — come out. I have only seen Holly shed a tear once and it came grudgingly. That was when we were at the site where the Twin Towers once stood in New York City. If I hadn't been there to witness it, I would never have believed it. Seeing Holly's tears gave me hope — gives me hope — for her future. For in her tears, she will begin to find healing.

What's worse than carrying extra weight is how Holly views herself: dirty, awful, and horrible. She loathes herself, though you would never figure that out by talking to her. She looks into her soul and sees something evil lurking — something dark, dismal, that is at her core. Since this is her reality, how could she view herself in any other way but appalling and disgusting, thus unlovable by herself, others, and God?

Of course, nothing could be further from the truth. God cherishes Holly. I do, too. I cherish her because I see who she really is: someone created by God with unique qualities. Holly is one of my closest friends. She has that title because she is pretty, funny, easy to be with and a great photographer. With her, I can be me. When I am with her, I forget about my own painful experiences from childhood. I forget my insecurities, my fears, the fact that I sometimes doubt God's love for me as well.

Holly is a wife and mother. She loves her husband and her three children with all her heart. She dotes on her children, sometimes too much, knowing that she will never allow what happened to her happen to them. She loves Starbucks and the Denver Broncos. And she loves me. What more could a friend want? What more could a friend be? I enjoy being with her just as much as anyone else in my life, if not more. I can be myself with her, which is a rare thing indeed. I am blessed to have her in my life. She is a one-in-a-million woman and friend.

I understand why Holly questions God. She's a Christian, but she wonders where in the world He was on those dreadful, evil days that her brother stole her innocence. I wonder the same thing, I have to admit. Why didn't God intervene? We know He has the power to. Why did He not save her? Just like everyone else in her life, He appeared to look the other way, to be silent, to just have been too busy on those days.

To Holly, the answers are obvious. She was not good enough to be saved. She's dirty. She's sub-par. She's inadequate. She's unlovable and unlovely. God, it seems, was occupied with more important things on those days than loving Holly; than taking care of His precious little child. She cried out to Him, but her cries fell on deaf ears. Didn't they?

Even though I empathize with Holly and understand, to a degree, how she feels and why she does what she does, I can never completely and totally get it. What I do get is her anger, her fear, her doubt, her addictions. I have a few of my own, after all. Deep down, she is so much more than she has become. She is a brown, ugly caterpillar waiting to be transformed into a beautiful, fragile butterfly. How I long for her to be set free from the ties that confine her living the mediocre existence that she does. She would love to be free, too, but has not yet embraced the pain or the demons that have been in control, up to this point, of her mind, heart, soul and body.

A day is coming when my fat friend will no longer be fat. She will shed the image she has of herself — the image she thinks God and others share — and she will be free. It's true, she will be thin. In fact, as of this minute, Holly has shed over ten pounds. But she will be so much more that that. She will be emancipated and uninhibited, finally able to be all that God purposed her to be. Isn't that so much better than skinny? It is, it really is.

From Pain to Peace
By Conita R. Marshall

The night started like any other. No top-breaking news stories. No massive destruction from the earth's elements. No major political issues that would affect the nation. Yet for me, it was not another typical night. In fact it was quite the opposite. For me it was the beginning of a whole new revelation. One that changed my life and my perception of it.

At sixteen and a ward of the state, my latest residency was a foster home. Like many teenage girls, posters of the hottest entertainers covered the walls of my bedroom. I had a decent bed and a compact stereo system. Except for the fact that it was not my permanent room, there was nothing too frightening about it. That is until that night.

Sleep had finally made its way to me and brought with it all the comforts of peace. But my rest was soon disturbed by an evil presence; a presence so strong that my eyes bolted open. Seconds later, my vision focused to see a dark shadow standing over me. Fear gripped me and restrained my movement. No sound escaped my lips. As he moved closer to me, my heart pounded faster and each beat seemed to echo through the room. I awoke with sweat seeping from every pore.

The earliest memory of my stepfather's molestation was at six years old. Until I was fourteen, I endured his midnight visits that escalated to penetration at the age of twelve. Like in my dream, I often awoke to him standing over me; my voice captive, as my mind tried to understand why I was subjected to so much pain.

This awakening had a profound impact that caused me to live and operate out of fear. Two years free from my molester, fear now held me captive. If he could enter my dreams, what was to keep him from entering my life again? The realization that I had indeed been a victim of molestation, versus a series of horrendous nightmares, set the stage for a life sentence of imprisonment within my mind. I did not experience the piercing sound of prison doors closing behind me, but the loud voices of negativity and fear reiterated my lack of safety.

The heinous actions of my stepfather seemed to open Pandora's Box to other perverts. Throughout my childhood and adult life, countless others sexually violated me. Each encounter made it more difficult to see life outside the four walls of my private cell. Walls of fear, violation, low self-esteem and loneliness were contained with the ceiling of anger and the floor of resentment.

As a young girl, I was introduced to the concept of being touched by a female. So by the time it happened again during my teens, I accepted it as part of the process. On another occasion, a female stranger enticed me with candy — a major lure to a first grader. When I followed her to the garage in the back alley, she told me to remove my clothes. At some point during this offense, she hurled bricks and pipes at my head. The physical scars still remain.

I cannot recall when the flashing neon sign that read "Do with me what you will" appeared across my forehead, but men also mistook me as an open invitation to violation. Numerous perpetrators raped and fondled me. Stores, buses, school, bars, you name it, I've been abused there. A simple walk down the street left me bleeding in an alley after an assault.

The thought of my body being valuable and worth protecting never occurred to me. How could there be any real value to something that was so battered? The more pain I felt, the more relief I needed. The mind can endure only so much before seeking refuge. My solace came through drugs and alcohol.

I tried my first joint in the eighth grade. One of my foster sisters later reintroduced me to marijuana and by my sophomore year, it became a part of my life. The drinking binges commenced soon after.

Still able to function in school, I maintained honor roll status and never viewed my actions as destructive. I convinced my softball teammates to quit smoking during the season. That meant I had to be in control, or so I thought. My senior year I only had two classes followed by work. I kept my grades up and even ran for class president. My top college choice accepted me and paid the entire tuition. In fact, I got money back. My drug and alcohol usage continued into my freshman year of college. And although I slacked in a few classes, I didn't see a need to change my behavior.

As an adult, I shunned away from sex. Prospects were there, I just had no desire to be sexually active. Each time the opportunity presented itself, the walls of my mental cell closed in on me. That is until I met a man who refused to take "No!" for an answer. I was almost twenty when we met. Not attracted to him, but flattered by his interest, I took his number. We went out a few times and then I decided that a relationship would not work. When I mentioned it to him, he convinced me to continue to see him as a "friend." We made plans to go to the movies. He picked me up as times before, but we did not go directly to the movies as I had expected.

"I've got a few stops to make," he said as he parked in front of a strange house. Over the next few hours, he visited several strange homes that were accompanied by equally strange individuals. A few men got in and out of the car throughout the night. I grew more frustrated because we still had not made it to the movies. Looking back, I think I was angrier at myself for not sticking to my guns and severing all ties with him.

At times, he left me alone in the station wagon as he made another "stop." By the time he got back in the car, I had had enough.

"Take me home!" I crossed my arms across my chest and huffed.

"Aw, baby, I'm sorry. I didn't plan to make so many stops and miss the movie." He leaned over and kissed my cheek. "How about we go somewhere special so I can make it up to you?"

I liked special treatment, so without much hesitation, I agreed.

The "somewhere special" turned out to be a park. Now given the right circumstances, with the right person, it could have been a wonderful evening, however...

He grabbed a blanket from the trunk and we made our way to a grassy hill. He spread out the blanket and motioned for me to sit. We talked for a while and then he introduced me to a pre-mo — a joint laced with cocaine — but couldn't get it to burn right. According to him, the two drugs were out of balance. All this unnecessary drama and I couldn't even get a decent high.

A few minutes later, a policeman told us that we had to leave because the park was closed. We went to another area and sat in the car to talk.

At some point we started kissing. Keep in mind that I was not interested in him, but got caught up in the attention. We moved to the back of the car and then I felt compelled to stop.

"I don't want to go any further," I said, as I tried to climb over the seat. He ignored my pleas and continued. "Stop it!" I

163

hit at his chest, but to no avail. I cried and screamed "No!" as he forced himself on me.

He jumped up. "Get dressed. I think the cop is coming back."

I sat up, adjusted my clothes and then sighed.

"False alarm. We're good. Lay back down." He pushed my shoulders.

"No, I think you better take me home. It's getting late." Thank God he agreed and we started home.

We rode in silence for the first ten minutes and then he said, "I think we're being followed." He peered out the rear view mirror. I looked out the side mirror, but at one in the morning, all I saw were two bright headlights; that is, until the red and blue lights flashed at us. We pulled over and parked under a streetlight.

He tried to hand me a small pouch. When I refused to take it, he threw it on my lap. I hurried to hide it before the officer approached. My mind raced back to when he bragged, "Yeah, I own every house we stopped at." The revelation hit me that he indeed was a drug dealer and I was an unwilling accomplice.

The officer shined the flashlight in our faces. "I need to see both your IDs." He used the beam of light to read our licenses and then he looked at the driver. "Step out of the vehicle."

I sat in the car while the officer ran our information. From the side mirror, I saw him put the driver in the back seat of the cruiser and then return to the station wagon.

"Ma'am, I need you to get out of the vehicle."

My turn to stand on the sidewalk, I palmed the pouch in my hand and watched as they searched the car. When they allowed me to sit back in the car, I took the first opportunity to hide the contraband.

"Here's your ID." I tucked it in my purse. "You're free to leave, but your date is under arrest. Can you get home on your own?"

My date? Not hardly "Yes, sir."

"Okay. Your date wants to speak with you."

I walked to the cruiser and leaned toward the window.

"Will you take the keys to my father?"

I had met his father on one of our previous "dates" and agreed to return the keys to him.

"Cool." He raised his voice to get the policeman's attention. "Excuse me, officer! Can you take her home?"

Before the officer could reply, I said, "I'm good. I can walk home. Thanks anyway." The walk to my foster mother's house took me about an hour. Since her granddaughter lived next door, I decided to go to her house.

I explained to her what happened with my "date." She took the keys and called her friend, a policeman, to take them to the station. She also told me to check my panties for blood. Here I was three months from my twentieth birthday, sexually violated numerous times and on course for years of a raging mental battle.

As I stated earlier, my body had no value to me so I mistreated my temple like others had done. Albeit a bit wiser, I committed to being the one in control. At times I practiced celibacy, not for religious purity, but because I got tired of the emptiness that followed the hollow encounters. I desired a meaningful connection, but knew better than to hope for anything more than routine interactions. I accepted my lot in life, and instead of holding out for a sincere, pure relationship, I settled for drugs and alcohol to numb the pain.

I searched for love, but found rejection and heartache instead. Even after accepting Jesus as my Lord and Savior, the fury in my mind continued. I could not comprehend why I subjected my body to abuse and what it would take to be released from the mental prison.

As I grew in the knowledge of the Lord, so grew my understanding of how much I needed Him. I attended church service often, asked questions, watched those individuals whom I thought were positive examples and searched the Scriptures. I found Scriptures that applied to my situation like Psalm 25:4-5 and Proverbs 3:5-6 which encouraged me to do things God's way and acknowledge Him in every aspect of my life. Through the years, the Scriptures rooted in my heart as I learned to see myself as God saw me. Psalm 139:14-18, Jeremiah 1:5, 29:11-14 and John 15:16 spoke about God's purpose and plan for my life before my birth and how He desires for me to grasp this concept and walk in it.

The more time I spent with Him and read His Word, the more I built trust in Him. Every part of my life that I gave to Him was provided for spiritually, emotionally and financially. My faith grew stronger along with my dependency on Him. I realized that I needed Him to live life to the fullest. Having all this knowledge, why then was I still "locked" in my mind's way of doing things? Following the same behaviors, patterns, and making the same foolish decisions? I was growing in the Lord, so why was I not growing in this one area?

I sought God about my struggle. He revealed that I had to be completely exposed and honest with myself to get the help I needed. The truth is I had given God every part of my life but this one. My celibacy — over and over again — did not mean that I had committed to God's way. I realized that I did not trust Him to give me my heart's desire; therefore, I tried to make things happen myself. I was tired of waiting on the Lord to bless me with a husband. Tired of watching my friends and others get married while I remained single. Why was God allowing everyone else to have a committed relationship and not me? "Oh, God, what have they done to be granted this gift that I haven't?" Some time later, He told me that I desired to be married more than I desired Him. Ouch! I applied Romans 12:2 to my life. I had such a love and appreciation for my Lord that I did not want to continue to put my desire to be married as an idol over Him. But two years later, after another failed relationship, I was once again in the same situation. I thought that I had finally pulled up the weed at the root, but realized that I had only scratched the surface. The demise of the last relationship was much harder to comprehend and caused me to reevaluate me.

Upon a deeper dig, I arrived at the true source of my self-imposed prison. Beyond not trusting God to bless me with a husband, I did not think that I was worthy to have an anointed man of God as my husband. Spoiled at an early age and then raped at nineteen, which resulted in pregnancy, I felt contaminated. Infected. So not only did I not have virginity to offer my husband, I also had "baggage" — marked by society, forever labeled by a scarlet letter. The stares and looks of disappointment upon the faces of my elders reaffirmed my mind's conversation of unworthiness.

Since they did not know, or even try to know, the source of my actions, the jury's deliberation came back as promiscuity. No one knew the ongoing turmoil my mind used to bind me especially with my sexuality as a woman — I felt "dirty" for acknowledging it. Yes, my mirror's image had been tainted by premature sexual exposure left to develop under its own devices.

Once I admitted this to myself and then God, the chains broke. When I repented for my disregard of my Master's Word, my vision cleared and the doors of my cell opened. The value of my body elevated to the value of my life. I understood why it is a gift to be shared only through the covenant of marriage. As I read Scriptures that pertained to sex, the guilt and shame vanished. Hope, joy and excitement replaced them. Why? Because I knew that God had restored the ashes of my abused, battered and torn body with beauty.

The gift of my body is so valuable that God's Word makes provision to protect and preserve it; to keep me from the dangers that lay in wait. So now when I think of my wedding night, I no longer think about the things I cannot give him because I have something to present to him — the gift of a free, healed and whole me. Not shattered pieces of myself, but the entire me as God created. No one else has ever, nor will ever, have this from me, until that day the Lord has set aside to change my last name. As for the so called "baggage," she too is just as precious and valuable.

I no longer cringe and avoid Scriptures that speak about purity and righteousness concerning the body because they are truth as I know it. I live Romans 12:1 and present my body as a living sacrifice, holy, acceptable to God because I value my body and my life. Precious! I read Scriptures that deal with freedom and assurance such as John 8:31-32, Romans 8:1-2, Hebrews 13:5 and Philippians 1:6 to help me stay focused and free. The prison walls of my mind have fallen and I have chosen not to rebuild them again because "whom the Son makes free is free indeed!"

Tainted Goods
By Sheila Reid

I understand why God says in His holy Word "It is better to marry than to burn." Weekly Bible study meetings taught me that this did not mean burn in hell, but that one's flesh would burn with an intense desire for sexual satisfaction. I had no idea how strong intense could be until I turned twenty-nine.

I gave into that burning desire. This seemingly uncontrollable yearning brought about my slow demise. I believed then and I believe now that God spoke to me and told me not to allow Sly to visit me on that dreadful MLK weekend that seemed like bliss at the time. Yet, against my better judgment, I allowed Sly to enter my home and my pleasure zone. I did not fully consider the consequences of my actions, but about a month and a half after Sly's visit, I was forced to accept them.

At my third visit to the doctor's office I had no idea what was wrong with me. My doctor was in the process of running a series of blood tests to discover the source of my fatigue. "Could you run a pregnancy test while you are at it, Dr. Lala?" I hoped that a developing life was not the source of my drained energy.

I must have been a twenty-nine-year-old idiot. Pregnancy was a concern, but not my only concern. Sly could have been with some stank female, from God knows where, before he left Cleveland to visit me. I could have contracted a horrific disease. *What was I thinking?*

I hadn't been with anyone for three years, not since I broke up with Wayne and moved to California. I wasn't supposed to do the nasty again until I was married. I tried to be a good girl.

Sly just had a way of making me feel so good. He awakened every desirable bone in my body.

"The pregnancy test is positive, Loyal," Dr. Lala said. I waited two hours to hear what I thought was the most devastating news of my life. I could not contain my emotions. My body shivered as rivers flowed from my eyes. I was pregnant by a man I trusted and for whom I cared deeply. I knew he felt the same for me. However, I was not in love with him, nor did I think he was in love with me. I failed my family, my church, my unborn child, God and myself. In a matter of a few short days, I had become something I never thought I would become — a statistic that fed into racist stereotypical mentality. I was now a single, black woman carrying a child and I was now, tainted goods.

"This isn't a good thing," Dr. Lala asked. "I thought you always wanted children."

"I did. I mean I do, just not this way. I was supposed to be married first. I don't even know if the father is in love with me. He lives in Ohio. I don't know what I am going to do. It was not supposed to happen this way."

"Do you want to explore other options?"

"I don't know. How much time do I have?"

"It must be done within your first trimester."

I left her office devastated. I never thought I'd be in a position where I did not want to have my child.

When I returned to my Long Beach condo, I drew my bath, disrobed, and slowly sunk into the hot steamy water. I sat for an hour thinking, praying and crying. I reminisced about an episode of *Law & Order* where a woman had died after her boyfriend had given her a tea that was supposed to naturally abort their baby. Unfortunately, the tea had an adverse effect on the mother as well. If I could just remember the name of that tea, then my problems would be over. But what if I killed myself after drinking the tea? The tea thing did not sound like a good idea, but maybe I could drink enough wine to cause a miscarriage. Yet, I had never heard of someone having a miscarriage from drinking too much alcohol. That might not work and I could end up delivering a deformed baby. The wine thing was not a good idea either. I considered causing myself to have a bad fall down the stairs at my apartment. A harsh fall would definitely cause a miscarriage. The problem with this was I could not bring myself to purposely fall down concrete steps. No, none of these ideas were any good. I got out of the tub and decided that I would follow proper medical procedure and have an abortion.

The next morning, I awakened to a news story about a young man fighting for his paternal rights. He had discovered that his girlfriend was pregnant and planning to have an abortion. He wanted her to have the child for him to raise. This guy actually wanted his child regardless of the mother's involvement. The unwed-mother-to-be felt that she had the right to terminate her pregnancy because the fetus was in her body and not her boyfriend's.

"Jeeeez, I wish I were in her shoes." This woman knew that the father of her child wanted their unborn baby so much that he was willing to take her to court to prevent the termination of her pregnancy.

Oh my God, I thought. What if Sly wants this baby and I haven't even given him the chance to tell me how he feels? It would not be right for me to have an abortion without knowing how he felt about it. I decided to give Sly a call. If he seemed uninterested in having this child, I would go ahead and terminate the pregnancy. However, if he appeared interested, I would have our baby and make the best of the situation.

171

"This is Sly."

"Hey, Sly it's me."

"Hey, did the doctor say what was making you so tired?"

"Yes, I'm pregnant." Tears poured down my face. I tried to hold them back as best I could. "We should have used something. I told you I wasn't on the pill."

Sly took a deep breath. "When you told me how drained you were, I figured you might be pregnant. What do you want to do?"

"I don't know," I sniffed back tears and tried to remain composed. "I don't believe in abortion, but---"

"Don't worry. It will be okay. I'll be out there in a couple of months and I'll support you. You know I was planning on moving out there anyway. I'll just come sooner."

I couldn't believe my ears. I expected him to encourage me to have an abortion. Yet he was so comforting. His calm soothing voice stayed with me the rest of the day and for many days to come. He called me every day to ask if I was okay and he kept me informed about his move to Long Beach. I couldn't wait for him to come. The more Sly called the more excited I became about seeing him again. I just knew everything would turn out fine.

When Sly made it to Long Beach, I was three months pregnant. My boobs were round full orbs; my tummy was firm and solid. While no one at work noticed my pregnancy, my hips had started to spread and I had to add maternity clothes to my wardrobe. None of this mattered because Sly embraced my body and made me feel like the sexiest woman alive.

Sly worked hard to get his investment business in Los Angeles off the ground. Unfortunately, he had several setbacks. His house in Cleveland did not sell. Clients were not coming as quickly as he had expected and he did not like the long fifty-minute commute from Long Beach to the outskirts of Downtown L A. I tried to make things as comfortable for him as possible. My income was steady so I knew that I could sustain us until things became more secure for him.

I wanted to make Sly feel comfortable and less stressed. I made sure he had a hot fresh meal waiting for him when he arrived from his long commute. The apartment was always neat with sweet scented candles burning each time he came home. My timing was generally pretty good. While the food was warming on the stove, I took my shower. When Sly arrived from his strenuous commute, I greeted him with a kiss in my most comfortable evening attire. No matter how I felt, I never turned Sly away.

I was now four and a half months along and barely showing. Most people at work still could not tell, but I could no longer get into my old clothes. I focused on preparing for the arrival our child. Sly had made a point of meeting Dr. Lala and being there for my check up.

"Loyal, I am going to be involved in this baby's life. I wasn't there for my first child and I'm not going to miss out again. I was not allowed to be in the room when Kyla was born. I am going to be involved and you never know what might happen. When things get a little better with my business, we may get married." Sly's sentiments gave me more comfort.

After Sly's comments, I made a conscience effort to include him in everything. I continued my monthly appointments with the chiropractor and massage therapist because Dr. Lala informed me that doing so would make my delivery smoother and less painful. I took a prenatal yoga class that met every Thursday evening. The class became my refuge. I prayed, meditated, stretched, relaxed and most importantly focused on my baby. I met other women who were naturalists like me.

From them, I learned about a natural birthing method that was more informative than Lamaze. It was called the Bradley Method and a class lasted for twelve weeks.

"Hey, Sly!" I excitedly crooned as I entered the condo after my Thursday night yoga class. "There's a natural birthing class called the Bradley Method. The first session is in two weeks. Class doesn't start until 8:00 so you can be back in time to go with me."

"I can't go, Loyal."

"Why? You're usually home by 7:30 and the class only meets once a week."

"Go by yourself."

Disheartened, I whined. "Who's going to coach me if you don't attend? You said you wanted to be involved."

"I just can't go.

"Well, there's a free baby and child CPR class at the hospital next week. Will you be able to go to that with me?"

"I can't go to that either. You don't need me there."

Crushed. He had been so firm about partaking in the birthing process that I just didn't know what to make of his comments. "Well Sly, I thought you wanted to go to these things with me. What would you like to do? I want you to feel like you're a part of this too."

"The baby won't be here until September. I don't know what you're so worried about. All you care about is the baby. I'm still trying to get my business off the ground."

I couldn't believe he could be so cold. I decided not to ask him to attend any more baby-related events. I would just keep him informed. To make matters worse, this became our first intimacy-free evening.

As time went on, I saw less and less of Sly. His cell phone was disconnected and I became concerned that I wouldn't be able to get in touch with him if something went wrong or I went into early labor. I offered to add him to my cell phone plan.

"I don't need a phone. You can call me at work."

"But sometimes I can't reach you at work, Sly. What if something happens and I can't get in touch with you? I can pay your bill until things get better with your business."

"You can call me at work. The baby's not due until September. You'll be fine."

Again, I could not believe my ears. I wished I had terminated my pregnancy, but now I was entering my fifth month and starting to show. I felt the baby move inside of me and abortion was no longer an option. Sly pulled away from me in disgust when I tried to wrap my arms around him in bed. Fear set in and the realization that I was tainted goods returned.

I looked forward to yoga class each Thursday night. It was a place for me to concentrate on positive energy. My friend, Armas, attended the birthing classes with me and I found him to be a tremendous support. I continued sessions with my chiropractor and massage therapist. I focused all my energy on the new life soon entering my world and I tried not to concentrate on Sly's inattentive manner.

"Hey, Loyal," Sly said after I answered the phone. "I won't make it home tonight. I'm just too tired. I'm going to stay here and sleep in the office."

"Are you sure you want to do that?"

"Yeah, I'll be fine. See you tomorrow."

"Okay," I hung up the phone. What else was I supposed to say? While it was possible that Sly could sleep in his office — it had a shower and pull-out leather sofa — I did not believe him. Several weeks had passed without our normal intimate evenings. I had to face the fact that Sly might be seeing someone else. The thought of life as a single mother horrified me.

I continued to pay all the bills and with the lack of attention from Sly, despondency entered my spirit. It had become too difficult to keep out the negative vibes that penetrated my soul. I no longer wanted Sly around unless he wanted to be here for our baby and me. I wrote him a letter and hung it on the refrigerator message board.

Dear Sly,

It appears that your feelings for me have changed. I feel used and betrayed. I've done everything I know how to keep our relationship strong for our unborn child and us. I know that things are still financially tough for you. However, if you are unable to give me the comfort and attention to maintain my emotional well being through this pregnancy, I would like for you to at least chip in for half the mortgage and utilities ($2,000). If this is something you are unable to do, we can talk about this further when you return from work.

Love, Loyal

Sly never came home from work. He didn't call and he was conveniently out of the office when I called. He still had clothes and furniture in my condominium so I knew that he would return eventually. I just didn't like the fact that he still had keys to my place and could come and go at will. I decided to leave work early and get the locks changed. Imagine my surprise when I entered the unit and found Sly packing his things.

"I thought you would have talked to me if you were going to leave," I said as I looked at the four or five suitcases scattered throughout the bedroom.

He continued to pack his suits into the garment bag. "Well, you told me I had to get out so I made things happen."

"I didn't kick you out," I walked over to the closet that was now half empty. "But obviously you're leaving. I don't know what I did to make you treat me this way."

Agitated with my presence, Sly breathed hard. He zipped up the garment bag.

"You're seeing someone else aren't you?"

"Don't worry about what I'm doing."

"Sly, you told me not worry. You said that you would support me and be involved. I trusted you, believed in you and supported you." I tried to hold back the tears, but the stubborn droplets flowed without restraint. "I have a right to know what's going on. I don't understand why you're leaving. I'm carrying your child."

"Well, when a woman tells me she's feeling used, I leave her pregnant or not!" With that, he slammed my keys on the kitchen table, grabbed his last bag and walked out the door. He has not returned.

I cried uncontrollably for over an hour. Bewildered, afraid and in a state of disbelief, I did not want to go on. I went to bed praying to die. I didn't want to live a life as tainted goods nor did I want my child to have a flawed mother for her only parent. Our destiny was now in God's hands. I believed He was punishing me for my inability to obey His Word and remain celibate until marriage.

I had set my affections on man and God wanted me to put Him first. He wasn't punishing me, but trying to get my attention to redirect my path. Although Sly has started another family, he is a good father to our daughter. She is flourishing in elementary school and enjoys swimming. I love being a mother and thank God for my little blessing every day.

Friday Night DUI
By Robert Muhammad

Friday night and I was going to see my friend's band perform at Katz, a local bar. I didn't want to drive way out to the suburbs because my license had been suspended. But it was Friday night, and I had a new car. Enough said. "I'll drive safe. Straight there and then to work." With two paper routes for the Dayton Daily News, I had to be at work between 3 and 4 a.m.

As an excellent and frequent "drunk" drinker, I'd never gotten a DUI or been involved in an alcohol-related accident. I can't exactly remember, but I had between ten to twenty beers — a daily habit for me at thirty-three years old — before I left for the bar. I arrived at Katz around 10 p.m. I met my friend, Eric, the band's light and sound technician, and he bought me a beer. Oh boy, Heaven. The opportunity to see my friend's popular band play at a sold out venue excited me. As their special guest and suited in my best, I looked good and felt better. I met new people, drank more beers. A great night.

My visit to the bar wasn't just for fun and relaxation. I had a hip-hop group and planned to use Eric's talents at my next event. He showed me the music set up and I was hyped. I called Robert, a member of my group with the stage name "Rated R." He and a friend were going to join me at Katz.

I introduced the guys and with my fifth or sixth beer in hand, we discussed our concert. Can you say, "Highly intoxicated?"

Robert and his friend were anxious to go to a new club in Centerville, a suburb about fifteen miles from Katz. The neighborhood contrast in driving from Dayton to Centerville is comparable to driving in New York City and then Mayberry. I had pushed my driving circle to the outer limits and didn't want to go any further, and besides I was already close to work. I had been to the club when it was Casablanca and knew it was a nice place. As a single man with a new car, I liked the female-to-male ratio. I wavered, but they talked me into going.

"Eric, I'll see you later. I'm gonna check out South Beach with Robert."

"Man, you be careful. I'll see you at work, right?" His concern was justified. He knew of my license situation.

To make sure I had vehicle access to get to work on time, I had them follow me. I stopped at a convenience store and got two more 24-ounce cans of beer. Now that I think about it, I was smashed.

I staggered into South Beach, and wow! A high-class club. Cool atmosphere, spacious, lots of neon lights and chrome. I love neon and chrome. I stepped into Miami, Florida as Don Johnson and switched from beer to liquor. I drank Pimp Juice. Bad choice. If you aren't familiar with hip-hop music, and the rapper Nelly, you're probably asking, "What in the world is Pimp Juice?" Well, it's Triple Sec, Malibu Rum and pineapple juice. I was dazed and confused. Looking back, I know I was sloppy drunk. With lights flashing and music bumping, I talked to various women and even danced with some.

We made it to last call and I stumbled out to the parking lot. I was work bound and drunk.

Robert came to my car. "Hey, man. I'm going to Denny's for breakfast with some lady friends of mine. Wanna join us?"

"S-Sure. I'll meet you there." No license and intoxicated beyond human possibility, I planned to drive ten miles further up the main street instead of hitting the highway a half-mile away. No problem, except that I failed to remember that Denny's had been closed for over four years.

About five miles up the road, westbound on State Route 48, I blasted my sound system. I glanced in my rearview mirror. *This is not happening.* Red and blue strobe lights danced in the mirror and I pulled over. How could this be? I revisited my check points. Seatbelts? Check. Driving within the speed limit? Check. Both hands on the wheel? Check. Use of turn signals? Check.

The state highway patrolman stepped back as he got a whiff of my breath. "Sir, step out of the car. I need you to take a field sobriety test."

Piece of cake. I had done this several times before. But this time, I stumbled and fumbled like a weeble-wobble. Somewhere in the back of my mind I knew this was going to happen; I knew that I needed this to happen.

Calm and relaxed, I cooperated with the officer as he escorted me to the cruiser. In route to the station, he even took me to Speedway because I needed to use the lavatory.

I spent about an hour at the precinct. They fingerprinted me, photographed me, asked me a host of questions, and of course, gave me a Breathalyzer test. Any drinking expert knows rule numero uno: always refuse the Breathalyzer test. But I wanted to cooperate. I also wanted to know just how drunk I was. The legal limit in the state of Ohio is 0.08. I registered at 0.18. More than double the limit, and it was probably a lot higher a couple of hours earlier.

The officer took me downtown to the County Jail. A million thoughts raced through my mind. I had to call my Mom and have her call my job. I had to ask for bail money which she didn't have. I faced a DUI charge, driving with a suspended license and no seatbelt — they threw that one in there.

Crap, I really screwed up. As head coach of my daughter's soccer team, I had a game at 2:30 p.m. I sat in jail all morning.

When you come to jail intoxicated, they keep you for a minimum of twelve hours. So even with my bail paid, I couldn't leave until around noon.

Mom had to work, so she asked her friend to pick me up. I got outside into the fresh air and beautiful sunshine, and felt miserable — the mental dumps. Somehow Mom's friend and I couldn't get into contact with each other, so I caught the bus home.

I walked in the front door and my senses were assaulted. My new puppy hadn't been let out for over twenty-four hours. Worn clothes strewn all over the floor. Dirty dishes piled in the sink. A full trashcan. The television blared. The bombardment was so intense that I could taste its grime. Yuck! I missed worked, felt terrible, and oh yeah, I had a soccer game.

I woke my neighbor and he volunteered to take me to the game. My team was excited to see me. We proceeded into our pre-game workout and won an exhilarating game. During the competition I had forgotten about the DUI.

I got my DUI in September 2003. With the help of an attorney, I avoided jail time by attending a 72-hour DUI intervention program. It began on March 18, 2004, a day after St. Patrick's Day.

~ ~ ~ ~ ~ ~ ~

Forward to March 2004. I almost died of alcohol poisoning fifteen days before the intervention class. Life's stressors had me bound for seven months. I got pulled over again and lost my job. Hopeless. Instead of facing my self-inflicted obstacles, I drank more.

Wednesday, March 2, I got stupefied drunk. I woke up on my couch, fully clothed. My head pounded like bongos; my mind, a perpetual blur. I was enrolled at Sinclair Community College. My worst hangover never kept me from school, but this one was different. I stumbled into the kitchen for something to drink. Nothing. I ate some peanut butter, I guess to settle my stomach. Bad idea. I crawled to the bathroom and vomited blood. The alcohol stupor did not suppress my fear. The dark red ooze petrified me.

Somehow, I made it back to the couch. The blood continued to spew from my mouth. I called my ex-girlfriend at work.

"Hey, it's me, Robert. I'm not feeling well."

"What's wrong? You sound terrible."

"Got an upset stomach. Can you bring me some 7-UP?"

"Yeah. Give me a few minutes to wrap this up and I'll be right over."

I hadn't locked the door, so she walked in to find me teetering between consciousness and oblivion. With my eyes rolled back in my head, blood ran down my face onto my shirt. She slapped me a couple of times and then called 9-1-1. The paramedics gave me oxygen and then whisked me off to Miami Valley Hospital.

Once at the hospital, the emergency room nurse gave me an IV. Still in my blood-stained long johns, dazed and confused, I continued to vomit.

"Why did you drink so much?" Doctors and nurses questioned several times.

"I d-don't know." That's it! Something triggered inside me. My sense of physical health stood and demanded that the mental anguish accept defeat.

I haven't had a drink since Thursday, March 4, 2004. I attended the alcohol intervention program with an open mind. I wanted help — needed help. I realized that I had been an alcoholic for twenty-two years. I learned the only way to solve my alcohol dilemma was absolute 100% abstinence.

Since I stopped drinking, I have accomplished a lot. Within one week of completing the DUI intervention class, I found employment. I made the Dean's list at Sinclair and graduated in the summer of 2006. I am forever grateful and thankful. That DUI is perhaps one of the best things that ever happened to me.

Valerie L. Coleman

Acid and the Good Shepherd
By Edward Acunzo

Have you ever talked to the Lord in a moment of doubt and fear? Of course you have. That's where you turn when you can't see your way clear. Have you ever had your prayers miraculously answered on the spot? No, I don't mean the question in the way that you're thinking. I'm talking about a face-to-face, heart-to-heart, personal discussion with Jesus Christ Himself, in the moment that you need Him most, when only He can save you.

As a teenager, like many misguided "seekers" of the 60s, I experimented with a wide variety of drugs, in fact the whole spectrum of what was available at the time: from marijuana and other mind-expanding drugs to the most self-destructive stuff like heroin. I had many near-death experiences in embattled Bronx streets, but none more terrifying than one single encounter with LSD.

I found the idea of acid quite frightening and intriguing at the same time, but I was determined to try it. Other friends were doing it, and somehow it seemed adventurous. My nickname was "Zero," and sometimes I felt compelled to live up to the billing. I found it amazing that five people could take the exact same dosage — or at least thought they did — of the same batch of the same brand of acid, and have five different reactions. I heard that acid had varying amounts of speed in the mix, and the more "speedy" the acid, the lower its quality — whether fact or myth, I don't know. But it seemed like some people had an incredible tolerance to acid and had minimal hallucinations, if at all, while others hallucinated wildly. For instance, a friend took two or three trips of "yellow sunshine." He claimed to see "trails" behind movements of things like

184

hands or fingers, or even rainbow trails of vivid colors, but no other hallucinations. I, on the other hand, could NEVER take two or three hits of any acid, that would be entirely too much for me. But I could take one hit of that same "yellow sunshine" and hallucinate like I had been sucked into a Walt Disney full-length cartoon having no basis in the reality taking place around me. In other words, I experienced the acid trip as a complete departure from reality and became part of a new reality. The acid trips could be amusement park enjoyable and funny, or scarier than anything Stephen King and Wes Craven together could imagine. The outcome was a total crap shoot each time.

LSD hallucinations can involve all five senses together, just a couple or none. A hallucination can take the form of an idea or a belief system; in a word, delusion. During parts of the trip, usually pre-peak and post-peak, hallucinations seemed to be controllable in frequency, intensity or even type. Other times, you had to strap yourself in for the ride and hold on for dear life, with no idea of where you were going, or whether you were ever coming back.

The uncertainty excited many people and was the main reason for taking the trip. They found it entertaining and mind expanding. That same uncertainty and loss of control frightened the mess out of me, but like an idiot, I took it anyway. Assessment of the quality of "trips" was simple for me. The ones that frightened me were "bad" trips; the ones that didn't and were enjoyable were "good" ones. Although I had a handful of good ones that were lots of fun, entertaining and had the illusion of mind expansion, I had more bad than good until I had one so bad that I was "cured" from acid curiosity. I'll tell you a little about both, starting with the good.

If you are stupid enough to risk taking LSD, which is like playing Russian roulette with your sanity, it's a good idea to trip with others — essential that it be people you trust, preferably one who is straight, but acid-experienced, and another who is tripping with you. The one tripping with you is sort of a playmate, and the other one is a guide if you find yourselves going off on a psychologically or physically dangerous tangent.

One time I violated these rules. I went home and tripped alone in my bed in the dark, which wasn't a particularly bright thing to do, but it wound up being a delightful trip. The darkness became a blank canvas upon which Disney characters came to life and played with me all night. Colorful, non-threatening and enjoyable. Not mind expanding, but it sure was fun.

My trips were always full of visual and tactile hallucinations, and sometimes delusions as well. On a mind-expanding trip, at least it seemed that way during the trip, I had companions and a guide. I believed that I was on a quest for the Holy Grail. Once I passed into the peak of the trip, awareness that my belief system was acid induced vanished. I was on an intellectual quest for encoded or encrypted information that was present somewhere in my neighborhood. And if I cracked the code, the information would reveal the answers to many of the mysteries of life. I searched all over for clues; most of it done by feeling. I read the surfaces of buildings and streets with my hands and fingers like Braille was written on them. I must have looked insane, ready for the butterfly nets, but it felt like I was doing important work for myself and mankind.

After a while I noticed a paisley-like pattern that appeared on the sidewalk. With great intensity, I studied it. It seemed to have rhyme and reason, but I couldn't crack the code. Then it occurred to me that involving multiple senses together was required. This theory excited me. I got on the floor, ran my fingers over the paisley patterns and tried to read them in a Braille-like way. At the same time, I tried to read them visually. With both interpretations combined, voila! There it was. Right in front of me. The answers that explained some of life's greatest mysteries!

I read for what must have been a couple of hours. Mystery after mystery was revealed to me. Immensely satisfying. I couldn't wait to share this information with the world. As I slipped out of the peak of the trip, my ability to read the code faded and the knowledge that I had gained also faded. By the end of the trip, the only knowledge that I retained was that I was filthy from crawling all over sidewalks and walls. I needed a shower and a change of clothes, but it sure felt great to know it all for just a little while. I guess my mind expanded and then contracted.

Then I experienced the mother of all bad ones, the last acid trip I ever took. It started off terrible, but it was too late to do anything about it. I had Saturday afternoon all planned. Do my chores early and then run some errands for my mother, the last one was to pick up the dry cleaning. I planned to take the acid tab and then drop off the clothes and groceries at the house. By that time, the acid would be coming on and I could meet up with my friends.

Everything ran according to schedule, the acid started to come on, just as I got home. But something was wrong. My Aunt Lily was there, which was unusual. Aunt Lily, my mother and one of her friends were in the kitchen crying. Dad was lying down in the bedroom.

"What's going on?"

"Your dad's been for his annual cancer check-up. They found evidence of multiple tumors throughout his body, including internal organs. They say it's inoperable." All three women cried. I knew I needed to stay with my family, but I had to get out of there before the acid kicked into high gear. An LSD trip can cause a fragile state of mind.

"I've got to be alone." I ran out of the house and took off into the street.

I found my friends and told them what happened. They were already tripping and my news bummed them out, so they ran from me like I had the plague. I began to peak and my reality shifted, so although I was still in my neighborhood, I had no idea where I was. Everything looked foreign as I stood alone. For all I knew, I was on Mars.

A big monstrous thing stopped and bellowed a huge, terrifying roar. "What in God's name is that?!" My eyes grew as big as saucers. Parasites rode on its back, and when it roared, they dismounted and fed it. They grabbed can after can of food and threw it into its mouth. He swallowed the food, but kept roaring for more.

Transfixed, I watched in amazement and fear. Will those creatures be able to keep up with its appetite? The parasites fed it more and then the beast seemed to be satisfied. It stopped chewing and roaring. I let out a sigh of relief, wiped the sweat from my forehead and leaned against the wall. The parasites jumped back on the beast as it rumbled down the block and then it stopped and roared again!

"Feed him and hurry up!"

The parasites worked furiously to keep it from going berserk and wrecking planet dwellings or eating the inhabitants. But the monster was insatiable; it couldn't get

enough. I felt like I was watching a train wreck in progress —
horrified, but could not look away. I followed in panic.

"If they don't feed him fast enough, he may decide to eat
me!" The parasites tired and I sensed that my end was fast
approaching. "Lord, please save me. I don't want to die." I was
gone baby, way out there in the twilight zone, when I noticed a
long-haired guy with a beard. He walked up to me and sat on
the fender of a parked car.

"Why don't you come over here, Ciro and have a seat with
me for a minute?"

"All right."

"Do you know who I am?"

I trembled. My voice quivered as I said, "You're Jesus of
Nazareth."

"That's right. Do you know what's wrong with you?"

"Yeah, I'm crazy."

"Yes, Ciro. But do you know why you're crazy?"

"No, Lord. Maybe because I'm bad.

With tears in His eyes, He said, "No, My son. It's because
you took a drug called LSD that has poisoned your mind."

I cried. "Can You help me, Jesus?"

He placed His hand on my shoulder. "If I give you back
your right mind, what will you do with it?"

"I honestly don't know, Lord. But I promise You I'll never
take LSD again as long as I live."

The Lord got off the fender and began to stroll away. He
looked back over His shoulder, smiled and said, "It's a deal,"
and then vanished.

I turned to check on the monster. Nothing, but a nasty, old
garbage truck and a couple of sanitation workers who stood on
the sidewalk next to it. They stared at me like I was crazy.

Not anymore, fellas. Calm replaced my panic.

Now you could dismiss this whole event as just another hallucination, just part of my LSD trip, but you'd be wrong. I'm as certain of this as I am that there is a God. I cried as I recounted this story, almost forty years after the fact, because every fiber of my being knows the truth now as I knew it then. At the most frightening moment in my life, when I was sure that I was insane and had no idea why, Jesus Christ Himself spoke to me. He gave me a second chance.

I wish I could say that was the last time I used drugs, but I don't want to lie. But it was the last time I ever used LSD or any other psychedelic drug. No, not me. I'll keep that promise until I meet Him again. I know when to keep up my end of a bargain.

About eight years later, He showed me the path to giving up the rest, but that's a story for another day.

The Face I See in the Mirror is Not Mine
By Pamela C. McColla

Some people find it difficult to look in the mirror. I'm not referring to the tempered glass that provides a reflection of physical appearance, but to the mirror of one's soul — the true reflection of thoughts, feelings and character. We try to avoid letting people see our weaknesses because such transparency leaves us vulnerable to their judgment and criticisms. Many of us do not face the reality of who we are because the intense self-analysis forces us to be accountable especially when we exhibit counterproductive behavior. I recently discovered that I was going to be accountable, if only to myself, if I expected positive changes in my life.

I awakened one morning and, as usual, thanked God for another day. While my thankfulness is genuine, and my faith is real, I realized that I was dissatisfied with my life. Not unhappy, but I definitely had a discontented spirit. I had not pursued my passions, cultivated good relationships or fulfilled God's purpose for my life. In addition, my professional aspirations had not peaked and my JOB — just over broke — not only fell short of my financial needs, but had become a source of chronic stress. I felt like I had held my breath for the last twenty years. I waited for someone to recognize my value and show me through the doorway to the accolades for my diligence. I didn't consider myself a total failure, but after a series of disappointments, I concluded that I needed to engage in self-reflection. I needed insight into why I hadn't gotten the results that I had worked toward all of my life.

Wise enough to realize that success would not be handed to me I worked hard to educate myself and develop business skills. I made sincere attempts to give a lot in relationships

191

because I expected to receive a lot. But I found that my professional opportunities were hindered primarily because of fractured relationships with superiors. I noticed a disjointed imbalance in my personal relationships as well.

But these matters were just symptoms of my problem. Not only was I dissatisfied with my life, but I had become angry about it. And at some point, my anger had seeped through my subconscious, into my thoughts, actions and interactions.

So how did I evolve into the person I had become? I saw the bumps and forks in the road, and I made some errors in judgment. But how did I end up on this path of perpetual discontent? I had to find out why I suffered from low self esteem. I wanted to understand why I overcompensated in my personal relationships, that is, gave and gave as if just being me was never enough. When did my pattern of antagonistic relationships with authority figures begin? When did I start masking my disappointment with anger? I needed to resolve these issues to be free from bondage, and experience a positive transformation.

I initially resorted to the 'pass the buck' mindset. It's much easier to point an accusing finger at someone else, so I developed a list of people who had maliciously blocked my progress. I got an epiphany when the Lord revealed that my focus was misdirected. Most of the answers to my problems were within me. Yes, the enemy was "in me." He allowed me to see that to understand my present state I had to retrace the steps of my past. I had to dig up roots that had been buried and overlooked for years. My anger did not sprout overnight, but festered underground from events that occurred years ago. He showed me that everything begins as a seed and the seeds of my discontented spirit were planted when I was a child.

I tried to recall experiences that may have contributed to my current flawed state and, surprisingly, remembered things from when I was as young as four years old. I remembered feeling happy and secure. As the youngest and only girl of three children, I felt protected. Our parents insisted that my brothers look out for me, and that we always stuck together. I was smart and thought I would be or do something big and important. I believed it deep in my spirit before I knew anything about God and His influence in my life. But He had already begun communicating with me, planting seeds of blessings and encouragement in my heart and mind that He would later harvest.

All living things have their origin in a seed and, at an appointed time, the fruit of that seed is harvested. We think of people, animals and plants when we consider this fact. Most people fail to consider that thoughts, feelings and relationships are living things, too. Our thoughts and feelings are fed and developed through seeds of exposure and education. Our relationships are birthed and nurtured through human interaction. Just as a gardener who wants fruit, vegetables or flowers plants the seed required to get the desired product, the kinds of seeds planted in us as children determine the kinds of adults we will become. This realization became the foundation of my journey toward changing some unfruitful patterns and habits.

I didn't remember any overt abuse or discouragement at the hands of my parents. My upbringing was typical for a mid-middle class family. No obvious dysfunctions. Both of my parents were in the home, and I was a daddy's girl. He planted good seeds in me — confidence, integrity, perseverance and strength. I learned these qualities through observation and his interaction with my brothers. My father was sick for about five years and then he died when I was sixteen. Just about the time I needed his guidance and could appreciate and acknowledge him for the strong man that he was, he was gone.

My mother was a dutiful, devoted wife. Through a combination of her Southern upbringing and the values that were instilled in her by her grandmother, she formulated a vision of family. Committed to maintaining an ideal family life, she insisted upon clean kids, a clean house and a home-cooked meal everyday. My mother was the epitome of femininity and grace and a stern disciplinarian; the living manifestation of the proverbial "iron fist in a velvet glove." She raised us to be well-mannered, respectful children, who did not question or challenge adults. At times, her practices and reactions were a bit extreme, but I admire and commend her for her steadfastness because, if nothing else, my brothers and I grew up to be civilized adults.

In spite of what seemed to be a maternal nature in my mother, something was missing in my relationship with her. The bond between a mother and her only daughter did not exist. Although I was aware of this gap in our relationship, I wouldn't define it until years later.

Both of my parents worked full-time jobs, so I was left in the care of my maternal grandmother. When I reflected on the memories of time spent with my grandmother, the associated feelings pummeled me. I spent most of my childhood hating her because of the fear she instilled in me. Regardless of my efforts to love and respect my grandmother, she said vile, unforgettable things to me, with little thought or hesitation. And since her venom was always directed at me — never at my brothers and never in front of my parents — I thought her attacks were strategic: to hurt me, to wreak havoc on my emotional and psychological development and to abort any possibility of my rising above the toxins she deposited into my spirit.

Her destructive influence stayed with me, despite my efforts to rid myself of its remnants through selective amnesia. A steady diet of her negativity and discouragement, which lasted about thirteen years, endured the test of time and overrode any positive thoughts of self-image. Yes, the conduit for the destruction of my healthy self esteem and natural progression toward fulfillment was my maternal grandmother.

When I recalled the disdain I felt for my grandmother, I remembered how I also resented the effect that she had on my family. At an early age, I told my father about her verbal attacks. When he confronted my mother, they got into a loud argument that escalated to the point of my father threatening to leave. The thought of him not being around, leaving me unprotected from my grandmother, was unthinkable. I never mentioned it to my parents again and found the strength to endure her abuse until I was old enough to move away.

The memory of the incident between my parents gave me insight into the division between my mother and me. In retrospect, it seemed that my mother was oblivious to my grandmother's mistreatment toward me, and that bothered me. Although my first attempt was futile, my posture and demeanor reflected how unhappy I had become. I developed a withdrawal defense mechanism to minimize attention to me and avoid verbal assault. The change in my behavior should have been obvious to my mother, but she never explored it. As a result, I developed a deep resentment toward my mother. I felt that she didn't love me since she chose not to protect me. These feelings intensified when, despite my father's vehement objections, she moved my grandmother into our home after he died. From my perspective, she intentionally put me in harm's way and that was unforgivable. I spent years resenting my mother which convinced me that my grandmother had succeeded in cementing my unhappiness.

With the unveiling of this revelation, I wanted to know why my grandmother and mother were the way they were. I pondered what had happened to them that caused them to develop into the women they were. Had my grandmother been violated or disappointed and the result was her bitter disposition? Why did my mother seem to overlook my grandmother's cynicism even when it was directed at her? Through conversations with family and indirect comments about past situations, I learned that a pattern of pain and discontentment had woven into the fabric of our family.

I came to understand that I was being victimized by the demons and latent emotional scars that had plagued my mother's family for years. My destiny was interrupted, almost canceled, by this family curse — "don't ask, don't tell, don't confront" — the curse of ignorance. A curse that developed as a result of old, Southern Baptist traditions that gave the outward appearance of living chaste, Christ-centered lives. But the posture was to avoid acknowledging deep, unresolved issues in the hearts, minds and spirits of relatives and extended relationships which permeated an indelible mark on future generations. As a result of this internal familial imbalance, I, along with a number of my relatives, suffered indescribable frustration, confusion and brokenness.

My grandmother had experienced emotional, psychological and perhaps, physical pain. Since her prideful perspective did not allow her to see a means of resolution, she methodically destroyed any potential nurturing, supportive relationship. The unfortunate result was that she never healed from the things that kept her bound.

When my grandmother died, I didn't feel anything. However, I was moved to compassion for my mother because she grieved deeply. Given the truth of their relationship, I found her emotions strange. But subsequent conversations with my mother revealed that she determined to love her mother, in spite of her meanness. While I was able to empathize with her choice, I struggled with it. In pursuit of her mother's love and acceptance, she forfeited a strong bond with me.

But God is great. He divinely orchestrates everything in our lives. After this revelatory journey through my past, God led me to a place of healing. He allowed me to see that I remained in bondage because I had not forgiven my mother or my grandmother. I carried the weight of such a heavy emotional burden that undermined my personal pursuits and attempts to have healthy relationships. He gave me the grace to move forward when I released this problem to Him. And when I slipped into a pity party because of the years wasted being angry and unproductive, He directed me to forgive myself. He helped me to see that some of the barriers I encountered prepared me for the ultimate destiny that He had for me. No testimony without a test.

My healing and deliverance enabled me to pursue my interests and follow my true calling. I enrolled in school to get a long-anticipated degree in counseling, and I found an opportunity to write and share my experiences with others. I've made changes in my communications and expectations of others, and I already see positive results. I found solace in the fact that my willingness to be transparent may help someone realize that they can heal and move on with their life, if they identify and confront their pain.

Now, when I look in the mirror, the face I see is mine. And I'm happy with what I see.

Second Chances
By Dianne Sagan

The twenty-passenger plane bounced over the Front Range headed west out of Denver. A cold front pushed south as we flew through partly cloudy skies over the Colorado Rockies. I hoped the Dramamine would keep my lunch down. After forcing myself to eat the sandwich, I didn't want to suffer losing it into a baggie.

Thankful when we landed in Grand Junction, I hurried down the steps, took my bag from the flight attendant and followed the other passengers into the small terminal. My eyes scanned the crowd, desperate for a familiar face. Six hours had passed since my last communication with the hospital.

Upon reaching the lobby entrance, I juggled my bags and fished for sunglasses in my purse. Searching the cars parked at the curb, I didn't see my daughter-in-law's Subaru. I heard my name and turned to see Jane, my son's mother-in-law, walking in my direction. My stomach churned and my mouth went dry.

She threw her arms around me and asked, "How are you? How was the flight?"

"I'm okay." Jane took my luggage and we walked to the car. "Where's Rica? I-is everything all right?"

"Let's talk in the car. We're only fifteen minutes from the hospital."

I brushed away tears with the back of my hand and swallowed rising bile. As we pulled out of the parking lot, the fresh air blowing in the open car window helped me refocus and calmed my nausea.

"You need to know that Brad's pretty beat up from the accident. I'm not sure how to prepare you for how he looks.

Rica's with him in the Intensive Care Unit. We can only spend short periods of time with him."

More tears. I struggled to breathe and looked at the mountains in the late afternoon sun. *I don't know if I can do this*, I thought, reflecting on the phone call at 1:10 that morning.

~ ~ ~ ~ ~ ~ ~

The telephone rang. I peered at the clock.

This can't be good. "Hullo," I said.

"Is this Dianne Sagan, mother of Brad Chappel?"

Cobwebs clouded my brain. "Uh, yes, it is." Not knowing how I got there, I realized I was standing by the bed in the dark.

My husband, Greg, turned on a lamp. "What's wrong?"

I shook my head.

The man on the phone said, "I am calling from St. Mary's Hospital in Grand Junction, Colorado. Your son had an accident."

My knees collapsed and dropped me onto the bed. I swallowed hard, my blood turned to ice water. "Is he all right?"

"He's stable."

It felt like an anvil sat on my chest.

"The doctors are with him. My name is Jeffery Collins, the charge nurse."

I forced myself to function. "He's a climber. Did he fall?"

"No. He was in a mountain biking accident. I don't know anything else at this time. I'll call you when we have more information. He'll be in surgery for several hours. If you want to speak with me, call this number." He gave me the extension.

"Okay," I said. He hung up.

"What happened?" My husband embraced me.

"Brad's in the hospital. He---" I cried uncontrollably in his arms. Finally, when my voice steadied I explained. "I have to go. I need to get to him." In shock, my body went on automatic pilot. When we called the airlines my brain made little sense of the information.

Greg took the phone from my hands and within minutes had made reservations for the earliest flight possible to Grand Junction. I packed my bags, not knowing how long I might be gone.

Nothing made sense to me. Everything in me wanted to curl up in a little ball and have someone tell me it was a mistake. I prayed with intention and total focus, "God, please don't let anything else happen to my son. Please don't let him die."

Not able to sleep, we made a list of people to call. First, my daughters, then my parents, and by 7:00 a.m. I called friends requesting prayers for Brad. We sent a mass e-mail to everyone else.

My husband encouraged me to eat something, but nothing sounded appetizing. I barely managed hot tea before leaving for the airport.

~ ~ ~ ~ ~ ~ ~

"We're here." Jane's voice broke through my heavy thoughts. She parked the car and we walked into St. Mary's Regional Hospital.

Still feeling light-headed and nauseous, I struggled to put one wobbly foot in front of the other, one long hallway after another until we reached the ICU.

We faced the double doors. I hesitated, whispered another prayer and then followed Jane as she pushed through into pandemonium. She paused. I looked to my left through a glass window. Brad lay on a bed surrounded by monitors, multiple tubes, IVs and a respirator. His face was so swollen that I almost didn't recognize him. I crossed the threshold into his room mechanically. Rica and I hugged each other with a silent desperation that spoke across our age difference.

A nurse entered the room. "I'm sorry, but you'll have to leave. You can come again at seven." Rica and Jane picked up their purses to leave.

I didn't want to go. I wanted to stay with my son. Tears filled my eyes. I opened my mouth, but no words came out.

"You're Brad's mother," the nurse asked.

I nodded.

She smiled reassuringly. "I know you just got here after traveling all day. If you'd like to stay with him, that's fine. We'll be changing shifts soon, and we'll be involved at the desk discussing cases. If he needs anything during that time, we will take care of it, so don't worry."

Alone with my son, I moved to the bedside. Everything felt surreal. I reached across the railing and took his hand in mine. Instinctively, I recoiled. His hand was icy and unresponsive. His whole life he'd had warm hands that held my cold ones. Now it was my hands that held life's warmth. I took a mental survey of all the monitors, where each tube connected and followed it to the location on his body. I held my breath with each hesitation of the ventilator. It made the only sound.

Brad's coma gave him the appearance of not really being there, but somehow gone, leaving his shell behind. *Like he's dead*, I thought, and looked at the monitors for reassurance.

Pulling the chair closer to his bed, my hands held his right hand through the railing. "Brad, I'm here. Mom's here." I told him about the call, the plane trip, his sisters, his nephew, what was happening at home, how much we missed him and my favorite books. I knew that talking to patients in comas helped them find their way to consciousness.

When I ran out of things to say I sat in silence. Thinking. Remembering. I had left his abusive father when Brad was seven years old. Even though counseling had helped us immensely over the years, Brad and I still carried some of the baggage that kept us from being as close as we could be. He held deep resentments toward me that had not been expressed openly. We never dealt with them.

For ten years, I had tried to be mother and father, which by the way is impossible. I was so busy being everything to everyone that I didn't meet Brad's ongoing needs of acceptance and feeling that he counted as much as his sisters. From my point of view, I thought I had done a good job of single parenting. I knew my son was not happy, but we didn't address the stronghold that held both of us captive — until Brad's head injury.

When it came time for me to leave him and join the others in the waiting room, I could barely pry myself away. I fought the powerful urge to hold him, as if in doing so I could keep him from going away. Dread crept deep inside me, fearful he wouldn't be there when we returned.

Shortly after I settled into the sitting area, Jane and Rica went to the hotel. They had been at the hospital for twenty-four straight hours.

A gray-haired doctor with tortoise-shell framed readers perched on his nose appeared in the doorway. Each family looked at him with anticipation. He glanced at his clipboard. "Is Mrs. Sagan in here?"

"Y-yes. That's me." I stood.

"Please. Sit. You've just arrived from....uh, yes, Texas. I'm Dr. Bailey, Brad's neurosurgeon."

My ears rang and mouth felt chalky. "How is he? His hands are so cold ---"

"Brad's in a coma. That's natural for a massive head injury. Our bodies protect themselves when massive or multiple injuries occur. The brain shuts down everything that it doesn't need to keep us alive and then the body can heal."

"How long?"

"It's hard to tell. With some patients, it can be a few days, others a week or two, and others. Well, we'll cross that bridge if we have to. We don't believe at this time you need to concern yourself with that."

I cried again at the doctor's implications. He reached for my hand and I saw compassion in his eyes.

"Let me give you a quick review of his injuries. It sounds bad, and it is. But it's amazing that he isn't worse. Thankfully, your son was smart enough to wear a helmet and pads."

I nodded.

The doctor cleared his throat. "The MRI revealed two contusions on the left frontal lobe of the brain, seven or eight on the right frontal lobe. He has deep abrasions and lacerations on his face and neck. Brad received over 200 stitches, but most of them the plastic surgeon put inside his mouth."

The details of his injuries struck me one by one like blows to my chest.

"In addition to the visible swelling, tests indicate internal swelling of the brain. We have a monitor and a cranial drain to control the pressure and fluid build-up. It appears he may have suffered hair-line fractures in his neck, so we will keep him in a neck brace until that condition is fully understood. He fractured eight thoracic vertebrae, T-9 being the worst."

I dropped my head into my hands, overcome.

"We'll know more about what he's able to do when he wakes up. If there is any good news in this, his fractures don't appear to have any effect on his motor skills, but again we

won't know until later. With massive head injuries, there are
unknowns that must be faced as he progresses in the healing
process. Any questions?"

"What about the respirator? Can he breathe on his own?"

"I can tell you that he was breathing on his own when he
arrived on the medivac yesterday. With head injuries, we put
patients on a respirator so the brain can heal itself instead of
using energy for bodily functions." He rose and patted my
shoulder. "I'll keep you informed."

How could I ever be strong enough to get through this and
assist my son in a long-term recovery? I wanted a second
chance to work through our past and restore us to a close
relationship. I prayed silently, thankful that he had survived the
accident, even though we were unsure about the future.

During the long days waiting for Brad to wake up, people
who had been strangers grew to know each other and each
patient's injuries. We became a loosely knit support group.
Twelve families shared the excruciating uncertainty of a
relative or friend with massive head injuries. Families
encouraged one another and shared their faith. We gained
strength from comforting each other. Brad was put on prayer
chains all over the world by friends and family.

In the middle of the seven weeks that I spent in Colorado
with Brad, I suffered a complete melt down. An emotional and
physical wreck, my speech turned to garbled, misplaced words;
an uncontrollable migraine pounded in my head and my eyes
stopped focusing. I arrived at a glaring conclusion. I can't fix it
this time. I can't heal his injuries. I can't mend our relationship
and break the old strongholds of our pasts. I realized that we
both needed to heal and completely surrender to God. I must
depend on His strength for us to find our way to restoration.

For the duration of his hospital stay, Brad progressed through developmental stages from toddler to teenager. He was then a six-foot-four, twenty-two-year-old *child*. For me, the experience was touching, frightening and a second chance at mending old wounds in our relationship. We shared the opportunity of shedding the last chains of captivity and building a better life.

Brad had me all to himself for the first time in his life. We faced the painful baggage we dragged around. He dealt with feelings about his injuries, his sisters, his grandparents, his father and my re-marriage after ten years of being a single mother.

After returning home, I realized that I had to trust in the Lord to finish the healing that He had started in us both. I wept through several months of Brad's silence, waiting for him to process the emotional side of his injuries and his past. When he had recovered enough, Brad called me on Mother's Day and we began to forge a new and healthier bond.

Brad's injuries have healed now, and while he still suffers from pain in his neck and back, our relationship is stronger and closer. A frightening thing, this brush with death — but what a gift it turned out to be for us.

Do Better
By Deena C. Miller

When you know better, you do better — or so the saying goes. Or is it more accurately stated: *When you know better, you try better?*

I remember a client I had a few years ago. She faced, for at least the second time, the removal of her children from her home. As my second time representing her, we faced the permanent termination of her parental rights. I reviewed the facts of her case and considered her history. One theme in her actions became quite clear. Her consistent errors revolved around her relationship choices. Time after time, she chose the wrong mate, which led to problems with substance abuse, which led to domestic violence, ultimately resulting in the entrance and continuous presence of Children and Family Services. She lived in a perpetual and vicious cycle.

I am sure that upon further exploration I would have discovered that my client had a less than stellar childhood. I am confident that although she was not happy with the circumstances of her life, she really did not know how to do any better. The cycle of abuse will continue to fester unless and until someone learns and implements *The Principles of Doing Better.*

I kept a copy of an inspirational article in my desk to give to clients caught in a whirlwind of self-destruction. I handed it to my client and talked to her about her life choices.

"Have you noticed a pattern in your life that has led to your inability to properly care for your children?" We both agreed that her over-preoccupation with relationships and poor decisions when it came to selecting a mate were the underlying theme in her present problems. "You have tried the man route, and frankly you have not been very successful at it. It is time you try something else."

She received my advice quite well, as she always did, and I prayed that she would apply our conversation.

As I wrote this essay, I thought of all the areas in my life to which my advice to my client applied to me as well. *Try something else.* According to another often heard saying "If you want to attain something you never had, you have to do something you never did." So, if you want to gain wealth, and your nine-to-five is not making you wealthy, then you have to do something you have never done. If you want to have a closer relationship with God and you know you have not obeyed what He has told you to do, you better do something you have never done. If you want to move past mediocrity and progress to a higher plane, you better do better.

Is doing better easy to accomplish? Speaking for myself, absolutely not. We often get ourselves in a rut. We don't want to change old routines; old habits. They are familiar and safe. In spite of all that, our old ways of doing things may become ineffective and limiting.

What is keeping you from being all God wants you to be? What is prohibiting you from living in your purpose? Why are you living beneath your privilege? Whatever it is, ask yourself, "Is _____ worth my continuing to exist in my present circumstance? Is _____ worth my not making it into the Kingdom of Heaven?" As Jesus more aptly stated in Mark 8:37; "Or what shall a man give in exchange for his soul?"

Whatever it is that is keeping you from reaching your destiny, let it go. How? By doing better. No ifs, ands or buts about it. We just have to do better. Trying is not enough. Drop the excuses. As my sorority sisters taught me, "Excuses are tools of the incompetent used to build monuments of nothingness. Those who specialize in them rarely accomplish anything."

This leads us into further exploration into why we must do better. Why must we deny ourselves that which we desire? Is it reasonable for us to strive for perfection? The answer, quite simply is to improve the quality of our lives here on earth and in the hereafter. Considering my client's situation, doing better than she had in the past would have resulted in the following: 1) the discontinuance of involvement from Children and Family Services, 2) continued sobriety from her drug of choice and 3) the greater possibility of achieving and walking in her purpose.

If we want to have life and life more abundantly, we must obey God. I recall a time when a friend of mine tried to get me to engage in a sinful act. Amongst the many reasons as to why we should live free from sin, I pointed out my belief that our blessings are directly tied to our obedience. My friend, undoubtedly motivated by selfish gain, argued that disobedience has nothing to do with the blessings you receive. On the contrary, the Bible is replete with Scriptures correlating our righteousness to our blessings.

Blessed is the man that feareth the Lord, that delighteth greatly in His commands. His seed shall be mighty upon the earth: the generation of the upright shall be blessed.

~ Psalm 112

The chapter goes on to say that "wealth and riches shall be in his house: and his righteousness endureth forever." I urge you to turn a deaf ear to those who try to dissuade you from doing what thus saith the Lord. Run from those who try to keep you from doing better.

So you say that you are doing the Lord's will, working earnestly to do better, but have not received your blessing. One of my sorority sisters was out of work for a number of years. God kept her and her son, despite her lack of income. Nonetheless, she grew sick and tired of being sick and tired. As a Christian, she knew the Word of the Lord. But she had grown weary and did not want to hear any motivational talk. Some folks she talked to inquired as to what she may be doing wrong in her life. She knew she was living right and really could not understand why the Lord was taking so long to bless her. I told her that I would keep her in my prayers. She was happy to hear such a brief comment. To explain what God was doing in the life of my Soror, He was teaching her how to have greater patience and giving her a testimony to help others. Although she was doing all she knew to do, her test was one of patience, long suffering and faith in God. We can never stop striving to do better. We can always learn something more to make us better followers of Christ.

So what about the unjust, who seem to be blessed beyond belief, but are not following God's commands? Why are sinners blessed but often the righteous have to walk a straight line to stay on course? At first glance, this imbalance just does not seem fair. Personally, it seems that before I can even enjoy the pleasures of sin for a season, God steps in to redirect my course. Because God does not want me to get too far away from my purpose. He is not going to allow me to waddle in my sin. Praise the name of the Lord!

We must remember that God rains on the just and the unjust (Matthew 5:45). However, He gives the righteous wisdom to save us from the ways of the wicked. He expects us to stay on the good, straight path (Proverbs 2). Do not concern yourself with the blessings of the wicked, as their evilness will ultimately lead to destruction. Despite how appealing sin may look, stay on the right path. When you see the prosperity of the wicked, do not allow your feet to slip. We must draw near to God (Psalm 73) and He will bless us according to His riches in glory.

As Christians, we have no choice but to do better. According to Matthew 5:48, "we are to be perfect as our Father which is in Heaven is perfect." So, trying to be perfect is simply not enough. We have to go forth with an attitude of accomplishment. I will become drug free. I will flee from temptation. I can do all things through Christ. I am an over comer. I will, I must and I have to do better. Speak accomplishment in your life today.

Journal of Affirmation

Today, I will do better with respect to

_____

_____

_____

_____

_____

_____

_____

_____

_____

_____

_____

Where Do I Go from Here?
By Valerie L. Coleman

Several years ago, Bishop Marva L. Mitchell asked me to be the speaker for a Project Impact graduation ceremony. Project Impact-Dayton (ProjImpactDayton.com) is a not-for-profit agency committed to "equipping children and their families for success."

Some of the graduates had lost custody of their children, while others struggled to obtain a GED. I wanted to encourage them to look beyond the current circumstance and envision a victorious future. My notes for that presentation are below:

1. Guard Your Thoughts and Words
Be Careful
Be careful of your thoughts,
    for your thoughts become your words.
Be careful of your words,
    for your words become your actions.
Be careful of your actions,
    for your actions become your habits.
Be careful of your habits,
    for your habits become your character.
Be careful of your character,
    for your character becomes your destiny.
—Author unknown

o The power of life and death is in the tongue
o Stinking thinking kept children of Israel in wilderness for forty years
o Words can either build up or tear down
o Vision is future thought
    ❑ Project yourself from where you are today, to where you want to be
    ❑ Envision yourself there, in that place. Close your eyes and grab hold to the vision. See yourself as

the best student, parent, spouse, employee. Getting your GED, college diploma, dream job.
- ❏ It's not about how you feel today or your current situation. Speak life to it. Call it forth like Jesus called Lazarus out of the tomb. "Diploma, come forth."
- o Unlock the power of your mind
  - ❏ Believe in your heart and trust God
  - ❏ Conceive in your thoughts and words
  - ❏ Achieve by action
- o Take control of the things in your life you can control, your thoughts and your tongue.

2. Set Goals
- o Now that you are thinking on the things that are true, honest, just, pure, lovely and good (Phillipians 4:6-8)
- o And you have your thoughts in mind, speak them out loud, write them down and get to work (Habakkuk 2:2).
- o Set expectations for yourself and your children.
- o Write down your goals and keep them in front of you. Post them on the mirror. Read it and speak to it everyday. "I want to be a nurse."
- o How do you eat the elephant? One bite at a time. Take a long-term goal — becoming a nurse — and break it into short-term goals.
  - ❏ Research the field for opportunities
    - o Talk to someone in nursing
    - o Library or internet research
  - ❏ Visit a college Admissions Office
  - ❏ Enroll and attend classes
  - ❏ Obtain work experience as a volunteer or for pay
- o Reward yourself as each goal is reached, no matter how small.
  - ❏ Mail yourself a congratulations card
  - ❏ Enjoy a sweet treat, movie or gift

3. Develop a Support Network
- o Tell others your plans to create your atmosphere for success. The right people will

- ❑ Encourage and believe in you
- ❑ Monitor progress with your goals and help you stay on track
- ❑ Check you when you say you can't and jump start you when you say you ain't
- o Find a mentor. Someone who is where you want to be to give you advice and guidance. If you want to be a doctor, hang with a doctor. If you want to be a millionaire...
- o Stay away from negative folks, aka 'The Haters.' Either from guilt, embarrassment or pressure, they will try to deter you. It's easier to pull you back than to pull themselves forward.

4. Believe in Yourself
- o When all else fails, believe in yourself. Situations will arise that are outside of your control. Plans change and knock you off course. That's okay. Regroup and get back on track.
- o Pygmalion effect is a self-fulfilling prophecy. In other words, what I expect I will become, I will become. What you speak over your life and your children's lives will manifest. So,
  - ❑ Imagine yourself in nursing scrubs
  - ❑ Envision yourself as the boss on the job
  - ❑ Picture yourself receiving your diploma. With your cap and gown, strutting down the aisle, blow kisses to your loyal supporters and then take a bow.
- o Look in the mirror and talk to yourself.
  - ❑ "I can do this."
  - ❑ "I am special."
  - ❑ "God loves me."
- o Life is a series of choices
  - ❑ You choose to do right or wrong
  - ❑ You choose to believe or doubt
  - ❑ You choose to succeed or fail

And today, you chose to succeed. Now find a mirror, look at yourself, pat your chest, smile and say, "I am fearfully and wonderfully made. There's no one else like me in the world. And for that reason I am worthy to be loved."

About Valerie L. Coleman

Valerie L. Coleman has been called to help writers get their books published. Walking in her purpose, she established **Pen Of** the **WritER** or **POWER**.

Valerie has coached hundreds of aspiring authors through the process of writing and publishing. With a heart to teach and serve, she founded the **Pen To Paper Literary Symposium** in 2004. Past presenters include national best-selling authors Dan Poynter, Lynnette Khalfani, Vickie Stringer and Kendra Norman-Bellamy. In 2005, Valerie co-founded **Write On! Workshops**.

Valerie compiled and edited *Blended Families An Anthology*. The book has received international recognition as it addresses the unique demands of stepfamilies. Valerie travels the nation presenting *We are Not the Brady Bunch!* in an effort to help families.

In May 2006, Valerie took her writing and publishing curriculum to the prisons. In addition, she developed **Passionate Pens**, a writing program for high school students.

Eager to invest in joint collaborations, Valerie is a founding member of **Soul of the Pen**. The objective of this cadre of Christian authors is to use the written word to develop healthy relationships and strengthen families. Partnering with Dr. Vivi Monroe Congress, she formed **Queen V Publishing** to transform manuscripts into polished works of art.

Valerie is the booking manager and business liaison for **Christopher Entertainment Group**.

Valerie has a bachelor's degree in industrial engineering from GMI Engineering & Management Institute and an MBA from the University of Dayton. She is a college mathematics instructor. A mother of five, she resides in Dayton, Ohio, with her husband, Craig. They worship at Revival Center Ministries, International.

About the Contributors

Edward Acunzo was addicted to a variety of drugs from 1968 until 1977. After the birth of his son, he detoxified and entered a two-year in-patient therapeutic community. Upon graduation, he was hired by Odyssey House in New York as a counselor. He was later promoted to program director of the New Orleans facility where he held several positions before transitioning into the manufacturing industry. Acunzo is securing agent representation for his unpublished memoir. *Acid and the Good Shepherd* is his first published work.

Jessica D. Allen is an aspiring doctor and author. She strives to keep God first in her life and desires to use writing as a means to touch the lives of youth and adults across the nation. She is a senior at Thurgood Marshall High School and plans to pursue a career in pediatrics. In addition to being a Passionate Pen, she plays piano and dances for Vision Mime Team. Jessica is an active member of the Total Youth Gang at Revival Centers Ministries, International. *False Identity* is her first published work. The full novel, published by Pen of the Writer, releases May 2008 (ISBN-13: 978-0-9786066-2-6). PenoftheWriter.com/Ppen_Jessica

Amanda C. Bauch, writer and teacher, resides outside of Jacksonville, Florida. She has an MFA in creative writing from Lesley University and is working on a young adult novel and a memoir. She placed second in the 2006 Lantern Books Essay contest. Above all things, Amanda loves the triune God and tries to live her life in a way that pleases Him.

Erin Di Paolo is a freelance writer who lives in Denver, Colorado. She has a degree in technical journalism from Colorado State University (1985). She has been married to John for eighteen years and has three children: Joseph (15), James (13), and Alessandra (10). Her passions are God, writing, traveling, spending time with family and friends, and running. Her goal as a writer is to encourage others while learning to embrace those who are different from herself.

215

Veronica A. Grabill grew up in Chicago and attended Northeastern Illinois University. She received her master's degree from Christian Life School of Theology and is working toward her doctoral degree from Beacon University. Veronica was ordained by Pastor Claude Robold of New Covenant Church in Middletown, Ohio and is licensed by the State of Ohio. Veronica mentors young ladies incarcerated in Warren County Juvenile Detention Center. Veronica is married to Vic and they have four children. *Incarceration of Juveniles* is her second published work with Pen of the Writer.

José Omar Gutierrez, who prefers to be called Omar, is an aspiring doctor. He contributes to the community through Volunteers of America and his church, Santa Clara Apostolic Temple. A native of Mexico, Omar and his four siblings have endured many hardships. Not willing to let life consume him, Omar pulls from the negative experiences to fulfill his passion to write and draw. In addition to participation in the Passionate Pens program, Omar studies advanced drawing and painting to sharpen his creative skills. Omar is a senior at Thurgood Marshall High School and he is also enrolled in Sinclair Community College. *Darkest Days, Brightest Hopes* is his first published work. PenoftheWriter.com/Ppen_Omar

Red Handed, thirty-four years old at the time of writing, was raised in Columbus, Ohio. He is serving a fourteen to thirty-five-year sentence with the Ohio Department of Corrections. His submission, *Traits of a Man* was inspired by I Corinthians 13:11 as it refers to doing away with characteristics of a babe. After much soul searching and drawing closer to God, Red admits that his traits as a child carried into adulthood and got him into trouble. *Traits of a Man* is his first published work.

Cathy Joulwan lives in Middletown, Delaware. She was married to Chaplain Charlie who served over thirty-one years as a prison chaplain for death row inmates. Chaplain Charlie went to be with the Lord in October 2006. Cathy is moving forward with the ministry, currently serving as information coordinator for Prison Outreach of Delaware, as well as an independent coordinator for several other ministries. Cathy and Chaplain Charlie have one son, Rob. *A Page from My Journal* is Cathy's first published devotional in a book.

Meta E. Lee is a freelance writer. Her stories have been published in Sun and Shade Magazine, Traveler's Tales, The Miami Herald, countless other publications and the short-story collection, *Stories from the Heart.* She has been awarded first place and honorable mention in numerous writing contests. Now a retired school librarian, she is an active member of the Broward County Storytellers' Guild. She tells original stories and traditional tales to audiences ranging from preschoolers to senior citizens to inmates.

Charles E. Loper, III was born and raised in Delaware. He is a management technology major at Ohio University and has two novels scheduled for publication. Charles is loved by his kids; mother, Cheryl; father, Charles, Jr.; sisters, Dollicia and Dongerette; and his long time love, Atoya Tyree. He was on the road to destruction, until the Lord set his life straight. Now the only road he follows is Righteous Boulevard. Charles attended the Passionate Pen writing workshops at Dayton Correctional Institution. *A Pilferer and a Habitual Liar* is his first published work.

Charles Loper, III
4104 Germantown Street
Dayton, OH 45417

Christopher D. Lyttle uses both spoken and written word to convey his passion for self expression and revelation of God. His fervor for creative writing began in elementary school, however in 2002, his writing escalated to a higher level of excellence. Christopher has written hundreds of poems and short stories and hopes that God will continually bless the ink of his mind to flow freely. Christopher is a senior at Thurgood Marshall High School and attends Zion Hill Missionary Baptist Church in Dayton, Ohio. Also a Passionate Pen, *Where is God?* is Christopher's first published work. PenoftheWriter.com/Ppen_Chris.

Joy Marino graduated from the University of Cincinnati with a bachelor's degree in psychology and a minor in dance. Marino is a veteran of the United States Air Force. She has been a high school Spanish teacher for seven years and currently resides in Ohio with her husband and two daughters.

Conita Marshall was called into the ministry in 1994 while attending E.S.C.L.A. Ministries. She became co-director of Safe House for Women in Recovery where she oversaw women suffering from drug/alcohol abuse. Her first book, *The Stolen Gift,* releases soon. It deals with sexual abuse and how to utilize the Word of God for healing. Conita has two other book projects underway. *From Pain to Peace* is her first published work.

> Conita Marshall
> PO Box 31353
> Dayton, OH 45437
> Conita_Marshall@hotmail.com

Pamela McColla has a B.S. in business management and she is working toward an M.A. in counseling. She recently decided to pursue her lifelong passion of writing, and is completing her first novel. Her first published work, *The Face I See in the Mirror is Not Mine,* will serve as the foundation for her upcoming memoir.

Deena C. Miller is on the brink of her purpose with several literary works in the making. A self-proclaimed nutritionist and physical fitness enthusiast, her upcoming books delve into these areas. Miller has a bachelor's degree in criminal justice from Bowling Green State University and a juris doctorate degree from Ohio State University. A licensed attorney and mother of three, she resides in Stone Mountain, Georgia with her husband. *Do Better* is her first published work.

Halee Ann Montgomery and her husband, Tim, have three grade-school-aged children. The family is active at their church and Christian school and proclaims that God is the center of their lives. Halee is a computer systems analyst. She aspires to be a prayer intercessor and desires to encourage others to pursue Christ. *His Promise* is her first published work.

Robert Muhammad is president and CEO of Robert Muhammad Economic Empowerment, Inc., home of Creative Solutions Institute, a motivational speaking business; Rilex Professional Insurance Services and Supreme Bean Coffee Shop. Robert has an A. A. degree in communication arts from Sinclair Community College. He helps others reach their full potential by speaking from his experiences. Robert is an active member of the Nation of Islam and resides in Springfield, Ohio with his wife and four children. *Friday Night DUI* is his first published work and the prelude to the full-length book.

Economic Empowerment, Inc.
PO Box 10815
Dayton, OH 45402
RobertMuhammad.com   rwmuhammad@gmail.com

LaMont "B.I.G. Fridge" Needum is from Short North in Columbus, Ohio. He is the founder of Short Side Publishing. He authored two novels: *Straight Savage,* the first book of the *Short North Trilogy* and *The Short Side Blues*, which will be available in 2008. *To Each His Own* is his first published work.

Short Side Publishing
PO Box 35
Columbus, Ohio 43216

Adele Nieves is a writer, journalist, blogger and speaker. She earned her A.A.S. in international business from Berkeley College and her B. A. in communications/broadcasting from Seton Hall University. She is writing her first book, *What We Think: Gender Roles, Women's Issues and Feminism in the 21st Century*, and co-partnering in the production company, Liquid Words Productions. She will attend Sarah Lawrence College beginning Fall 2008 in pursuit of her M. A. in women's history. LiquidWordsProductions.com

Sheila Reid began working as a high school English teacher over twelve years ago. Her first full-time position as an educator was for Toledo Public Schools. She moved to

California where she continues to educate youth in South Central Los Angeles. Ms. Reid writes a column for mothers in *Virtue Magazine* and offers copyediting and tutoring services through her home-based business, Delightful Writing. She may be contacted via e-mail at delightfulwriting@yahoo.com.

Brian Revere, born in Middletown, Ohio, is currently serving time for a 2004 manslaughter case. The father of three, he is a revered artist with a passion for writing songs, screen plays and poetry. He attended the Passionate Pen writing workshops at Dayton Correctional Institution. *Deception* is Revere's first published work. Following his release, he will publish a book of poetry.

 Brian Revere 478-622
 4104 Germantown Street
 Dayton, OH 45417

Raised in Texas, **Dianne Sagan** writes editorials, short stories and flash fiction. She is a successful ghost writer. Her works in progress include Women's Bible studies, a series of suspense novels and Christian fiction. Dianne is a Sunday school teacher, choir member, Women's Ministry Bible Study facilitator, and a Small Group leader at her church, Hillside Christian Church. A member of Panhandle Professional Writers, she can be contacted at DGSagan.Tripod.com.

Kimberly Scott is a faithful member of Solid Rock Church in Monroe, Ohio. Under the leadership of Pastors Lawrence and Darlene Bishop, she has developed into a mighty woman of God. Her ministry to children has blessed many. She resides in Dayton, Ohio. *For Better, For Worse, For Prison* is her first published work.

Larry Sells writes personal essays, novellas, devotions, sermons and religious articles. He has published seventeen books filled with poetry and short stories available at Lulu.com/DeathWalk. Larry resides in Cedar Falls, Iowa.

Michael "Knowledge" Steptoe is a native of Springfield, Ohio. He has spent the past six years paying his debt to society.

He reports that knowledge of self manifests wisdom; wisdom shines upon the stars of understanding and nothing creates a state of certainty more than knowing who we are. Steptoe has had several poems and prose published. *The Jewel of Purpose* is his first published short story.

James Turner, from Dayton, Ohio, is serving a ten-year sentence in the Ohio Department of Rehabilitation and Corrections. He is a new-submissions reader for Triple Crown Publications and had two articles published in the Dayton Weekly Paper in 2004. Upon his release in 2009, James plans to pursue a career in publishing.

Charles "Chill Will" Williams is an Ohio inmate serving the remaining two years of his prison term at Dayton Correctional Institution. He was raised in Cincinnati, Ohio and has one child. He is an Ohio University English major and has written two unpublished manuscripts. *Identity Thief* is urban street lit based on a portion of his life. His goal is to become an established editor and romance novelist, depicting tales of love and devotion. Chill Will attended the Passionate Pens writing workshops at Dayton Correctional Institution. *The Seed of Karma* is his first published work.

Charles Williams 447-916
4104 Germantown Street
Dayton, OH 45417

Pen of the Writer

*Out of Ephraim was there a root of them against Amalek; after thee, Benjamin, among thy people; out of Machir came down governors, and out of Zebulun they that handle the **pen of the writer**.*

~ Judges 5:14

Pen Of the WritER

A Christian publishing company committed to using the writing pen as a weapon to fight the enemy and celebrate the good news of Christ Jesus.

Taking writers from pen to paper to published!

Pen of the Writer, LLC
PMB 175 – 5523 Salem Avenue
Dayton, Ohio 45426
937.307.0760
PenoftheWriter.com
info@PenoftheWriter.com

Passionate Pens

In 2006, Valerie L. Coleman developed a writing program for high school students and inmates. Under her tutelage, students learn the art and business of writing with the objective of completing a novella. She hopes to incorporate scholarships from accredited institutions as the pinnacle of the **Passionate Pens** program. **PassionatePens.com**

Jessica D. Allen, José Omar Gutierrez and Christopher D. Lyttle, contributors to *Tainted Mirror An Anthology*, are the first students to complete the one-year program.

False Identity
By Jessica D. Allen

Jasmine Jones despises the rising of the sun. It reminds her that she's still alive and has to face another day. Her mother's abandonment plunged her into premature womanhood and saturated her heart with bitterness. At fifteen years old, she turned her back on God and conformed to the world's standards. Will she make her way back to her first love or stay on the path of self-destruction?

False Identity is the first novel published under the Passionate Pen imprint of Pen of the Writer.

** Available May 2008 **
ISBN-13: 978-0-9786066-2-6
PenoftheWriter.com/Ppen_Jessica

Pen to Paper Literary Symposium

If you desire to put your thoughts on paper or you have already put pen to paper, this symposium is for you. Aspiring writers, published authors, book club members and anyone with a passion for literary work will gain insightful knowledge during this intense event.

The Art of Writing

Mainstream and self-published authors will step you through the process of writing. Genre-specific topics and general sessions will help you hone your craft and catapult your literary works to the next level.

The Business of Writing

Seasoned experts will provide practical tools to establish, manage and promote your book business. Attorneys, agents and publishers will enlighten and inspire you to pursue your life passion.

Throughout the day, attendees will have access to printers, editors, web designers, graphic artists and an on-site bookstore. One-on-one critiques by professional editors will give you personalized feedback about your manuscript.

For more information, send inquiries to
Pen to Paper Literary Symposium
PMB 175 – 5523 Salem Avenue
Dayton, Ohio 45426
937.307.0760
PenoftheWriter.com/PentoPaper
info@PenoftheWriter.com

The Doorway to YOUR Destiny!

Manna for Mamma: Wisdom for Women in the Wilderness

By Dr. Vivi Monroe Congress
ISBN 13: 978-0-9748020-4-6

Manna for Mamma: Wisdom for Women in the Wilderness links the similarities between the Israelites' journey from captivity in Egypt toward freedom in the Promised Land of Canaan, and the ten most common experiences women face today during their personal pilgrimage: Beauty & Aging, Dating & Marriage, Education, Employment & Finances, Illness & Death, the Missing Man, Parenting, Position, Religion and Self-Esteem.

This book responds to the wilderness conditions in a woman's life by revealing that Jesus is her manna, available to both sustain and deliver her. **Manna for Mamma** will inspire women to move in the direction of His promises for her life, already fulfilled and awaiting her arrival.

"**Manna for Mamma** answers the hows and whys that come in those hard pressed, seasons of pruning and testing. Dr. Congress is bearing literary fruit to nourish us all!"
—Norma Jarrett, J.D., Author of *Sweet Magnolia* (*Essence* Book Club Selection)

For information on bulk order purchasing or to schedule author appearance, visit **DrViviMonroeCongress.com** and **MannaForMamma.com**

Gospel music has been described and influenced by many cultures and styles from church to hip hop and even funk. The new era of spiritual soul, a musical genre in itself, is being introduced by the eccentric sounds of the male trio, *Christopher*. Consisting of Christopher McNeal, Christopher Reid and Christopher Surratt, the trio has managed to reflect their raw and uncut perspectives of the Christian journey through their music. Their heart-felt lyrics touch upon real issues that people who love Jesus deal with on a day-to-day basis. Their newest release, *The Journey,* has a little something for everyone.

"Christopher's music is a refreshing break from the commonplace gospel fare. Their music bridges the gap that exists between praising God inside the church and the reality of leading a Christian life in today's world."
—Shawn Harrison, BKA Waldo from *Family Matters*

"With the strong fusion of old church integrity and boldness with a new kingdom vision; these brothers are going to storm the world with *The Journey*. I have no doubt that this CD will encourage souls from the sanctuary to the street corner!"
—Izzy, national recording artist

For booking, contact
Christopher Entertainment Group
PO Box 60461
Dayton, Ohio 45406
937.307.0760
MySpace.com/SpiritualRealSoul
ChristopherMusic.com
info@ChristopherMusic.com

Blended Families An Anthology

With divorce, single-parent households and family crises on the rise, many people are experiencing the tumultuous dynamics of blended or stepfamilies. Learn biblical principles and practical tools from award-winning authors, Kevin Wayne Johnson, Vanessa Miller and Dr. Vivi Monroe Congress. Edited by Valerie L. Coleman, *Blended Families An Anthology* ministers to the needs of those hurting and crying out for answers.

"No one can give a better perspective of blended families than one who has a first-hand account. In this eye-opening anthology, a wealth of talent combines with a wealth of experience and the end result is heartwarming, empowering and inspiring!"
—Kendra Norman-Bellamy, national bestselling author of *Crossing Jhordan's River* and *In Greene Pastures*

"*Blended Families An Anthology,* edited by Valerie L. Coleman, is chocked full of advice, experiences, and good old fashioned common sense that will be a blessing to anyone faced with blending families in today's diverse society."
—Idrissa Uqdah, author and reviewer for BAHIYAH Women's Magazine

A real account of life in a stepfamily because we are **not** the Brady Bunch!

** Quantity discounts available for family ministries **

Available at Amazon.com and fine bookstores everywhere!
(ISBN-13: 978-0-9786066-0-2)
PenoftheWriter.com/BFAA

Donations

Donations to distribute free ***Tainted Mirror An Anthology*** books to inmates are tax-deductible. Make payments by money order payable to "Passionate Pens."

Requests

Inmates may contact their prison chaplain, librarian, teacher, counselor or warden to request books for their facility. Prison staff and volunteers may write to the address below to request free or discounted books for inmates.

Single Copy Purchases

Single copies of ***Tainted Mirror An Anthology*** may be purchased for $17.95 which includes the cost of shipping and handling ($14.95 plus $3.00 shipping). Proceeds from book sales will be applied to the Passionate Pens Scholarship Fund. The money will be used to teach writing and publishing to high school students and fund the free/discounted books supplied to prison inmates. Send your payment by money order payable to "POWER Anthology" to

Pen of the Writer
PMB 175 – 5523 Salem Avenue
Dayton, Ohio 45426
937.307.0760
PenoftheWriter.com/Tainted
info@PenoftheWriter.com

Also available at Amazon.com (ISBN: 978-0-9786066-1-9)

Include your name, complete address, phone and email with all donations and requests.